MOUTHWATERING

Vegan BURGERS

MOUTHWATERING
Vegan BURGERS

Plant-Based Patties, Rolls, and Condiments

Chef Toni Rodríguez

Photography by Becky Lawton

Translation by Allison Hauptman

Skyhorse Publishing

MOUTHWATERING VEGAN BURGERS

Skyhorse Publishing books may be purchased in bulk at special
discounts for sales promotion, corporate gifts, fund-raising, or
educational purposes. Special editions can also be created to
specifications. For details, contact the Special Sales Department,
Skyhorse Publishing, 307 West 36th Street, 11th Floor, New York, NY
10018 or info@skyhorsepublishing.com.

Skyhorse® and Skyhorse Publishing® are registered trademarks of
Skyhorse Publishing, Inc.®, a Delaware corporation.

Visit our website at www.skyhorsepublishing.com.

10 9 8 7 6 5 4 3 2 1

Library of Congress Cataloging-in-Publication Data is available on file.

Cover design by David Ter-Avanesyan
Cover photography by Becky Lawton
Interior photography by Becky Lawton
Translation by Allison Hauptman

Paperback ISBN: 978-1-5107-7108-6
Hardcover ISBN: 978-1-5107-0554-8
eBook ISBN: 978-1-5107-0559-3

Printed in China

Contents

Veganism and vegan burgers

The first time I saw a vegan or vegetarian burger was in 2002. My sister had just become a vegetarian, while I never wanted to so much as look at a vegetable. She used to buy dense, hard veggie burgers from the nearby health food store that were nothing like the products offered today. After trying one once, I thought I could never be a vegetarian.

Much has changed since then. Most of the vegetarians and vegans I know love to cook. They experiment in the kitchen, working on making rich and delicious recipes for burgers, sausages, pies, croquettes, and more. There is a much wider variety of ingredients used to make products like veggie burgers, including whole grains, vegetables, and proteins. In the eleven years that I have been a vegetarian, I have tried hundreds of different kinds of veggie burgers: grilled, fried, baked, raw, made from vegetables, grains, legumes, seitan, tofu, tempeh, or mushrooms. I have seen veggie burgers made by friends, in restaurants, or made in my own kitchen.

I have tried plenty of burgers, especially recently. Even many companies in the meat industry are producing veggie burgers to try to enter this market.

Health-conscious consumers are refusing to eat meat because of the way animals are treated. We are experiencing a major change in our diets. Many people no longer see vegan burgers the same way I saw them in 2002. They see something appealing and tasty and are curious to try them when they see them on a menu in a restaurant.

If you search for "veggie burgers" online, you'll be surprised to see how many sites feature vegetarian or vegan recipes. You'll also see veggie burgers in many upscale restaurants, topped with vegan dressings like a soymilk-based mayonnaise without egg. For example, the Iglesias brothers of the restaurant Adria (leaders in modern cuisine) offer a veggie burger made from mushrooms. Even hamburger cookbooks feature vegetarian recipes. If I had been told in 2003 about the international popularity of veggie burgers, I would not believe it. I cannot even imagine what kind of change we may see in the next few years.

In Spain, we can find some delicious vegan burgers at Gopal, Cat Bar, Ale-Hop, B13, among others. These restaurants not only feature vegan burgers, but also other snacks such as tortillas, vegan potato croquettes, empanadas, and cakes. As I write this book in 2014, I know that we will see many more vegan burgers featured in restaurants in major cities across the country. Restaurants such as Shake Shack, Hard Rock Cafe, Home Burger Bar, Gobu Burger, and La Royale serve very interesting sandwiches for vegetarians and vegans.

The vegan lifestyle and burgers are totally compatible—we just don't use any ingredients with animal origins.

What is veganism?

Veganism is a lifestyle based on respect for animals. It is not just a diet but a way of life in which we avoid all items that depend on the exploitation of animals. Therefore, a vegan individual will not consume products that have been made from or tested on animals, does not attend shows where animals are harmed (circuses, rodeos, bullfights, cockfights), does not wear any clothing made from animal products (leather, wool, suede), and does not eat any animal products (meat, fish, eggs, milk, honey).

How can we prevent animal suffering? Today there are many brands of cosmetics that do not experiment with animals, there are circuses where no animals are exploited, and we can find many synthetic materials that are of good quality and have less environmental impact than leather or wool, for example. A vegan diet is very simple because it is a diet based on fruits, vegetables, whole grains, and legumes. All of these ingredients can be found in your local market. Other products such as tofu (made from soy), seitan (made from gluten), and tempeh (made from fermented soybeans) are low in fat and calories and provide many nutrients.

Reasons to eat veggie burgers

Eating veggie burgers has more advantages than disadvantages. The environmental impact is lower because water and grains are saved by not feeding livestock. Veggie burgers are made from whole grains and legumes. If all the grains currently used to feed livestock were used to make veggie burgers, we could provide food for many hungry people around the world. Furthermore, making veggie burgers does not exploit or harm animals, creating a safer world for them.

Veggie burgers are healthier than animal-based burgers. They are cholesterol-free, are good sources of protein, contain little fat, and can be made with a wide variety of ingredients depending on your preference: whole grains, legumes, seitan, tofu, tempeh, or vegetables.

Preparing vegan burgers

There are many ways to prepare vegetarian and vegan burgers. It is important to make sure they are moist and delicious. First, decide what flavor you want to create. You can make your burger from vegetables, grains, beans, or other plant products. To season your burger to taste more like meat, you can add pepper, herbs, spices, or smoked products such as smoked salt, liquid smoke, or smoked paprika, or you can actually smoke the burger yourself.

The second step is to get the texture right. If your burger is too moist, you can add bread crumbs, oatmeal, textured soy, or agar and calcium. You want your burger to hold itself together but still retain some moisture. Some burgers do not require the addition of a binder. Whole grains and vegetables can sometimes hold together on their own. Some ingredients, such as seitan, firm up as they cook. When following a recipe, it is important to pay attention to the recommended amount of binder to be added but also to observe the texture of your patty and judge for yourself. Many factors affect the texture of the patty—from the cooking process to the amount of water contained in the ingredients.

The third step is to choose a cooking method. Depending on the composition of the patty, burgers can be cooked with or without oil, deep-fried, baked, steamed, cooked in a broth, grilled, or left raw.

Follow the recipes carefully to create delicious burgers. The more you practice, the more comfortable you'll become gauging the correct texture and moisture content of the patties.

Utensils and special equipment

Burger mold: A circular utensil with a handle to press hamburgers into even, compact rounds.

Ricer: Used for finely mashing fruits and vegetables. It is ideal for making sauces, purees, and creams, and for mashing vegetables thoroughly to add to burger patties.

Peeler: For peeling fruits and vegetables. Also used for slicing vegetables into ribbons.

Bowl: A kitchen necessity for mixing and storing sauces, doughs, and any number of other ingredients.

Kitchen scale: For weighing ingredients. It is important to have one at home in order to more accurately follow recipes.

Knife: Chopping many ingredients is necessary to make burgers. It is important to keep your knife sharp to avoid accidents and to more efficiently chop ingredients.

Spatula: A flat metal spatula is best for flipping burgers and transferring them to bread.

Blender or immersion blender: For creating creams, sauces, or smoothies, or for chopping ingredients.

Ring mold: Aluminum ring used to shape burgers.

Tabletop fryer: For frying burgers and potatoes. Fitted with a basket to dip foods into the hot oil.

Griddle: A flat metal pan for even grilling.

Skillet: For sautéing or frying. Typically metal or cast-iron with low edges.

Chopper: A hand-powered tool used to efficiently chop produce, nuts, seitan, and all kinds of ingredients.

Mortar and pestle: Wood or ceramic bowl and hand grinder for mashing foods.

Common veggie burger ingredients

TVP (Textured Vegetable Protein): Made from soy protein extract, Textured Vegetable Protein can be found in various sizes. Small or medium flakes are best for making burgers. When soaked in water and rehydrated, TVP makes a great binder. It is a low-fat, high-protein ingredient.

Seitan: Made from wheat gluten, with a similar texture to meat. Seitan is simmered in a broth for added flavor. Seitan can either be added to supplement burger ingredients or act as the main protein.

Tofu: Made from soy milk, with a similar process used for ricotta cheese. The milk is simmered with an acid to separate the liquids and solids. The liquid is strained off, and the solids are pressed into a mold and left to firm up. Tofu comes in many textures and flavors: soft, hard, silken, smoked, spicy, etc. It is a very healthful addition to a veggie burger.

Tempeh: Made from fermented soybeans. Tempeh originated in Indonesia, where it is fried, grilled, roasted, sautéed, marinated, or eaten raw. It is rich in protein and calcium.

Legumes: Many legumes are commonly found in the kitchen, such as beans, lentils, chickpeas, soybeans, and peas. They are a wonderful ingredient to use in veggie burgers, adding a variety of flavors and textures. They are a good source of protein and carbohydrates.

Whole grains: Common whole grains used in cooking include wheat, rice, barley, spelt, millet, corn, and oats. They are a good binder for veggie burgers as they are very absorbent and rich in carbohydrates and protein.

Bread: Can be made with many different grains and an infinite combination of nuts and seeds. Bread can be shaped in loaves or buns and is even useful once it is stale as it can be chopped and blended into breadcrumbs, another useful ingredient used as a binder for burger patties.

Soy milk: Made from water and soy. Soy milk is very versatile and used in all areas of vegan cooking, including the production of tofu. It is great for making creamy sauces and even mayonnaises.

Vegetable oils: Made from pressed seeds, such as olive, almond, walnut, sunflower, peanut, sesame, soybean, or corn. They are wonderful for frying, making sauces, sautéing, etc.

Herbs: Plants used in cooking primarily for adding flavor. Herbs commonly found in the kitchen include: rosemary, thyme, basil, chives, oregano, bay leaf, tarragon, parsley, and cilantro. Some are commonly found dry, while others are best used fresh.

Spices: Plant-based ingredients used as condiments. Common spices for cooking include: cinnamon, paprika, saffron, cumin, ginger, turmeric, and cloves. Spices are key for flavoring burgers and sauces.

Mushrooms: A fungus that grows in wet environments. Some mushrooms are edible while others are poisonous. The most commonly used mushrooms in the kitchen are: shiitake, cremini, milk caps, portobellos, and porcini mushrooms. They are delicious in burgers, salads, and sauces. They contain no fat and are rich in minerals.

Root vegetable: A vegetable that grows underground. Potatoes and sweet potatoes are varieties of root vegetables that are very common ingredients in cooking.

Dried fruits and nuts: Nuts are a great source of fat; common varieties include: almonds, walnuts, pine nuts, hazelnuts, peanuts, and pistachios. Dried fruits contain lots of vitamins; common types are: raisins, figs, dates, and apricots. They are great when used in burgers, sauces, and side dishes and can be fried, roasted, or eaten raw. Soaked nuts are very useful for making creams, pastes, and milks.

Gelburger: Made by SOSA from sodium alginate and calcium. Gelburger is a binder used to hold ingredients together without the need to incorporate breadcrumbs, oats, starches, TVP, or anything else that would normally be used to absorb moisture. For example, you could sauté diced mushrooms in oil, let cool, and stir in the Gelburger to make a firm burger patty. Be careful not to use too much, or you might get a gelatinous texture that is undesirable in burgers.

MOUTHWATERING Vegan BURGERS

NOTE

All of these recipes make 8 burgers each.

Black bean burgers
with pico de gallo and chipotle mayonnaise

10½ ounces black beans
1 clove garlic, minced
1 red onion, minced
12 ounces seitan
¼ cup chopped parsley
¼ cup chopped cilantro
1 tablespoon paprika (smoked, if possible)
1 tablespoon oregano
olive oil
salt and pepper to taste
⅜ cup breadcrumbs

1. Mash the black beans in a bowl with a fork. Add the minced garlic and onion. Place the seitan, parsley, and cilantro in the bowl of a food processor and chop finely.

2. Add the paprika, seitan mixture, oregano, olive oil, and salt and pepper to the black bean mixture, and mix until the ingredients are all well blended. Little by little, stir in the breadcrumbs. Mix by hand until the mixture holds together.

3. Form eight patties, and cook them in a pan with a little oil over medium heat.

To assemble the burgers:

soft burger buns (see appendix)
chipotle mayonnaise (see appendix)
lettuce
black bean burgers
pico de gallo (see appendix)

1. Slice the buns in half and spread chipotle mayonnaise on both halves. Top the bottom halves with a few leaves of lettuce, then the burger patties, followed by the pico de gallo on top. Finish with the top bun.

2. Heat the burgers for a few minutes in the oven at 400° before serving.

Chorizo burgers
with eggplant caviar

To make the burgers:

½ cup TVP
water, or vegetable broth
15 ounces white beans
3 cloves garlic, diced
2 tablespoons sweet red pepper, diced
¼ teaspoon ground cumin
olive oil
salt and pepper
⅓ cup breadcrumbs

1. Soak TVP in water or vegetable broth until well hydrated. Strain to remove excess liquid.

2. Put the white beans in a bowl and mash with a fork.

3. In another bowl, mix the garlic, sweet red pepper, and ground cumin with 1 tablespoon of olive oil. Add mixture to the beans.

4. Add TVP and mix until well combined. Add salt and pepper to taste. Little by little, stir in the breadcrumbs until the mixture holds together.

5. Shape the burgers. Heat a griddle over medium heat with a little olive oil. Cook burgers on both sides until heated through.

For the eggplant caviar:

eggplant caviar (appendix)
½ teaspoon sesame oil
2 tablespoons nutritional yeast
¼ teaspoon nutmeg

1. Mix the eggplant caviar with sesame oil, nutritional yeast, and nutmeg.

To assemble the burgers:

ciabatta bread
extra virgin olive oil
8 mushrooms, thinly sliced
spinach leaves
chorizo burgers
eggplant caviar (appendix)
basil leaves

1. Slice ciabatta bread open and brush oil on both sides of the bread. Layer the mushroom slices on the bottom halves.

2. Top the mushrooms with a few leaves of spinach, then the chorizo patties, topping with the eggplant caviar and a few leaves of basil.

Lentil and smoked tofu burgers
with red peppers

To make lentil and smoked tofu burgers:

1 clove garlic | 1 onion | ½ teaspoon oregano | ½ teaspoon paprika | 1 teaspoon Dijon mustard | 1½ cups cooked lentils | 7 ounces smoked tofu | ¼ cup breadcrumbs | salt and pepper | olive oil

1. Add garlic, onion, oregano, paprika, mustard, and half of the lentils to the bowl of a food processor, and pulse until finely chopped. Add mixture to a medium bowl.

2. Grate smoked tofu and add to lentil mixture.

3. Mix in the rest of the lentils, breadcrumbs, and salt and pepper to taste, and mix until it forms a compact but moist dough.

4. Shape the burgers. Heat a griddle over medium heat, adding a little olive oil and cooking burgers on both sides until cooked through.

For the tomato-garlic bread:

8 slices country bread | 1 clove garlic | 4 tomatoes | extra virgin olive oil | salt

1. Grill the bread, or toast in the oven at 350° F for 5 minutes. Peel the garlic, and rub on the toast. Cut the tomatoes in half and rub on each slice.

2. Serve with a splash of extra virgin olive oil and salt.

For the peppers:

**olive oil
8 sweet red peppers | salt**

1. Put a skillet over medium heat with a splash of oil. Wash the peppers with a little water, add to skillet, and sauté for 5 minutes with a pinch of salt.

To assemble the burgers:

**pico de gallo (appendix)
tomato-garlic bread
peppers
lentil and smoked tofu burgers
mayonnaise (appendix) | chives**

1. Spread pico de gallo on 4 slices of bread. Split the peppers and lay flat on top of the pico de gallo. Place the burgers on top of the peppers.

2. Finally, add a tablespoon of mayonnaise with a sprinkle of chopped chives.

Lentil and walnut burgers
with rosemary pesto

To make lentil burgers:

¼ cup walnuts
½ cup TVP
water, or vegetable broth
¼ teaspoon ground cumin
½ tablespoon ketchup (appendix)
2 cups cooked lentils
⅓ cup breadcrumbs
salt and pepper to taste
olive oil

1. Preheat oven to 350°F. Toast the walnuts for 2 minutes.

2. Soak the TVP in water or vegetable broth until well hydrated. Strain to remove excess liquid.

3. Add the toasted walnuts, hydrated TVP, cumin, and ketchup to the bowl of a food processor, and pulse until well blended. Place the mixture in a medium bowl.

4. Add the lentils, breadcrumbs, and salt and pepper to taste to the mixture, mixing well to make a dense, moist dough.

5. Shape the burgers. Heat a griddle over medium heat with a splash of olive oil, and cook the burgers until browned on both sides.

For rosemary pesto:

3 tablespoons pine nuts
1 clove garlic
10 basil leaves
8 sprigs of rosemary, stemmed
½ cup extra virgin olive oil | salt

1. Preheat the oven to 375°F. Spread pine nuts on a sheet pan and place in oven, toasting until they turn golden brown.

2. Place the toasted pine nuts, garlic, basil, rosemary, oil, and salt to taste into the bowl of a food processor. Process until smooth.

To assemble the burgers:

soft burger buns (appendix)
sliced tomato
lentil and walnut burgers
mayonnaise (appendix)
rosemary pesto

1. Toast bread.

2. Top bread with a slice of tomato, then the burger, topping the burger with a tablespoon each of mayonnaise and rosemary pesto.

Moroccan burgers
with caramelized onions

To make the burgers:

2 cups TVP
water, or vegetable broth
3 cloves garlic, minced
½ cup parsley, finely chopped
2 tablespoons kebab seasoning
½ teaspoon ginger powder
olive oil
⅓ cup breadcrumbs
salt and pepper

1. Soak TVP in water or vegetable broth until well hydrated. Strain to remove excess liquid.

2. Mix the garlic and parsley in a bowl with the hydrated TVP, kebab seasoning, ginger powder, 1 tablespoon of olive oil, breadcrumbs, and salt and pepper to taste.

3. Shape the burgers. Heat a griddle over medium heat with a splash of olive oil and cook the burgers until browned on both sides.

For the caramelized onions:

2 red onions, thinly sliced
1 tablespoon brown sugar

1. Cook the onion slices in a saucepan over low heat with brown sugar for 10 minutes.

To assemble the burgers:

crusty bread
mustard
green lettuce
Moroccan burgers
caramelized onions
grilled potatoes (appendix)

1. Toast the bread on a griddle.

2. Spread mustard on the bread. On the bottom piece, layer lettuce leaves, burgers, and top with caramelized onions. Serve with grilled potatoes.

Mushroom and black bean burgers
with vegan cheese sauce

To make the burgers:

⅓ cup TVP
water, or vegetable broth
1 cup white mushrooms, diced
1 cup portobello mushrooms, diced
2 onions, diced
2 cloves garlic, minced
olive oil
1½ cups black beans
⅓ cup breadcrumbs
salt and pepper to taste

1. Soak TVP in water or vegetable broth until well hydrated. Strain to remove excess liquid.

2. Cook the mushrooms, onions, and garlic in a covered pan with 2 tablespoons of olive oil until as much liquid as possible has been cooked off.

3. Add the beans to a bowl (or mortar) and mash with a fork (or pestle). Add the hydrated TVP, mushroom mixture, breadcrumbs, and salt and pepper to taste. Knead to form a moist dough.

4. Shape the burgers. Heat a griddle over medium heat with a little olive oil, and cook the burgers until browned on both sides.

For peppers with sesame oil:

2 tablespoons sesame oil
4 bell peppers, thinly sliced | salt

1. In a wok over medium heat, warm the sesame oil.

2. Add the peppers and sauté with a pinch of salt until they start to brown.

To assemble the burgers:

soft burger buns (appendix)
dill mustard (appendix)
peppers with sesame oil
vegan cheese sauce (appendix)
mushroom black bean burgers
arugula

1. Warm hamburger buns for 1 minute at 350°F. Spread the bottom bun with mustard sauce.

2. Top bottom buns with peppers in sesame oil, then a few tablespoons of vegan cheese sauce. Place the burgers on top and garnish with arugula.

NOTE

Portobellos are a delicious variety of mushroom with a firm, dry texture and elegant taste.

Chickpea burgers
with garam masala and baked potatoes

To make the burgers:

2 spring onions
2 cloves garlic
2 tablespoons tahini
½ teaspoon ground cumin
2 tablespoons garam masala
½ cup chopped fresh cilantro
2 cups cooked chickpeas
¼ lemon, zested
1¼ tablespoons breadcrumbs
salt and pepper to taste
sunflower oil

1. Add the spring onions, garlic, tahini, cumin, garam masala, fresh cilantro, and ½ cup of chickpeas to the bowl of a food processor. Blend until well combined. Transfer mixture to a bowl.

2. In a separate bowl, mash the remaining chickpeas with a fork until crushed, but still chunky.

3. Add the mashed chickpeas to the seasoned mixture, along with lemon zest, breadcrumbs, and salt and pepper to taste. Mix well to combine.

4. Shape the burgers. Heat a griddle over medium heat with a little sunflower oil, and cook the burgers until browned on both sides.

To assemble the burgers:

soft burger buns (appendix)
romaine or iceberg lettuce
chickpea burgers
sour cream (appendix)
ground pepper
baked potato (appendix)
mayonnaise (appendix)
cilantro, chopped

1. Warm hamburger buns for 1 minute at 350°F. Top buns with lettuce and a burger, finishing with sour cream and pepper.

2. Open the baked potato, topping with a tablespoon of mayonnaise, and some chopped cilantro.

> **NOTE**
> Tahini is a paste made from sesame seeds; it's commonly found in Middle Eastern cuisine. Garam masala is a mix of spices used in many Asian countries.

Spinach and chickpea burgers
with grilled tofu and avocado

To make the burgers:

1 onion
1 tablespoon nutritional yeast
1¾ cup cooked chickpeas
2 cloves garlic, minced
olive oil
1 small bunch spinach, chopped
⅓ cup breadcrumbs
salt and pepper

1. Add onion, nutritional yeast, and ½ cup of chickpeas to the bowl of a food processor. Blend until well combined. Transfer mixture to a bowl.

2. In a skillet over medium heat, sauté garlic in 1 tablespoon of olive oil until it begins to brown.

3. Add spinach to the skillet, cooking for a few minutes.

4. Add cooked spinach to the chickpea mixture along with the breadcrumbs, remaining chickpeas, and salt and pepper to taste.

5. Shape the burgers. Heat a griddle over medium heat with a little olive oil, and cook the burgers until browned on both sides.

For grilled tofu:

16 tofu steaks
2 tablespoons soy sauce
pepper | 2 tablespoons sunflower oil

1. Season tofu steaks on both sides with soy sauce and a little pepper.

2. Heat a griddle over medium heat with a little sunflower oil, and cook the tofu until browned on both sides.

For avocado with lime:

4 avocados | 2 limes | salt

1. Cut avocados in half, and scoop out the flesh. Chop and set aside.

2. In a small bowl, zest and juice the limes. Add to avocado with a pinch of salt, and mash with a fork.

To assemble the burgers:

multigrain bread | lettuce | tomato | spinach and chickpea burgers | grilled tofu | avocado with lime

1. Toast the bread. Place a few lettuce leaves on the bottom slice, topping with one or two slices of tomato, burger, two grilled tofu steaks, and 2 tablespoons of avocado with lime. Add the top slice, and serve.

BBQ burgers with walnut buns

To make the BBQ burgers:

2 cloves garlic
1 tablespoon paprika
½ teaspoon powdered smoke (or oil smoke or smoked paprika)
1 tablespoon BBQ sauce (appendix)
1 tablespoon ketchup (appendix)
1¾ cups seitan (appendix)
1 cup TVP
water, or vegetable broth
⅓ cup breadcrumbs
olive oil
salt and pepper to taste

1. In the bowl of a food processor, add the garlic, paprika, powdered smoke, BBQ sauce, ketchup, and 1 cup of the seitan. Blend until well combined. Transfer mixture to a bowl.

2. Soak TVP in water or vegetable broth until well hydrated. Strain to remove excess liquid.

3. Add the hydrated TVP, remaining seitan, bread-crumbs, 2 tablespoons of olive oil, and salt and pepper to taste to the BBQ mixture. Knead until well combined.

4. Shape the burgers. Heat a griddle over medium heat with a little olive oil, and cook the burgers until browned on both sides.

For the quick ratatouille:

salt
1 eggplant, cubed
1 onion, diced
1 red pepper, diced
1 yellow pepper, diced
1 zucchini, diced
3 tablespoons olive oil
1 tomato, quartered, seeds removed
½ teaspoon oregano

1. Salt the eggplant, and set aside.

2. In a wok over high heat, sauce the onion, peppers, zucchini, and eggplant in olive oil until golden brown. Remove from heat. Add tomato, oregano, and salt to taste.

To assemble the burgers:

walnut buns | aioli (appendix) | quick ratatouille | BBQ burgers | BBQ sauce (appendix)

1. Warm buns at 350°F for 1 minute. On the bottom halves, spread a little aioli, and add 2 tablespoons of quick ratatouille.

2. Brush the burgers with BBQ sauce, and place on top of the ratatouille. Add the top bun, and serve.

Korean BBQ burgers

To make BBQ burgers:

**2 cloves garlic | 1 tablespoon paprika
1 piece of fresh ginger, peeled and grated
½ teaspoon powdered smoke (or liquid smoke or
smoked paprika) | 1 tablespoon BBQ sauce
(appendix) | 1¾ cups seitan (appendix) | 1 cup TVP |
water, or vegetable broth | ⅓ cup breadcrumbs | 2
tablespoons soy sauce | 2 tablespoons sesame oil |
salt and pepper | olive oil**

1. In the bowl of a food processor, add the garlic, paprika, grated ginger, powdered smoke, BBQ sauce, and one cup seitan. Blend until well combined. Transfer mixture to a bowl.

2. Soak TVP in water or vegetable broth until well hydrated. Strain to remove excess liquid.

3. To the BBQ mixture, add the remaining seitan, hydrated TVP, breadcrumbs, soy sauce, and 2 tablespoons of sesame oil. Add salt and pepper to taste. Mix well to combine.

4. Shape the burgers. Heat a griddle over medium heat with a little olive oil, and cook the burgers until browned on both sides.

For white kimchi:

**4 cups water | ½ cup salt | ½ napa cabbage, cored
and quartered | 1 small head bok choy, chopped
| 2 cloves garlic | 4 leaves of rosemary | piece of
ginger, peeled | 1 apple, peeled and cubed |
2 tablespoons sesame oil**

1. In a large pot over medium heat, bring water and salt to a simmer. Add the cabbage quarters and simmer gently until softened. Turn off the heat and add the bok choy. Let sit for 5 minutes, then strain.

2. With a mortar and pestle, mash the garlic, rosemary, and ginger.

3. In a wok over high heat, sauté the apple and cabbage with sesame oil, stirring in the garlic-ginger paste. Cook for 2 minutes.

To assemble the burgers:

**rosemary bread (appendix)
mayonnaise (appendix)
BBQ burgers
white kimchi**

1. Warm buns for 1 minute at 350°F. Spread the bottom buns with a little mayonnaise, topping with the burgers, and finishing with the white kimchi.

NOTE
Powdered smoke is a product that adds a smoky flavor to foods. Kimchi is a traditional Korean dish made with fermented cabbage and hot peppers.

NOTE

Sake and mirin are two products commonly used in Japanese cuisine. Sake is a delicious rice wine, and mirin is a sweet rice vinegar.

Japanese burgers

To make the Japanese burgers:

2 tablespoons soy sauce | 1 tablespoon sake | 1 tablespoon mirin | 1 tablespoon sugar | 1 cup TVP | water, or vegetable broth | 2 cloves garlic | 1 bunch fresh cilantro | 1 tablespoon freshly grated ginger | 1¾ cups seitan (appendix) | 1 teaspoon miso | ⅓ cup breadcrumbs | salt and pepper | sunflower oil

1. In a small saucepan, bring soy sauce, sake, mirin, and sugar to a boil to make teriyaki sauce. Remove from heat.

2. Soak TVP in water or vegetable broth until well hydrated. Strain to remove excess liquid.

3. In the bowl of a food processor, combine the garlic, cilantro, ginger, teriyaki sauce, and 1 cup of the seitan. Blend until well combined. Transfer mixture to a bowl.

4. To the teriyaki mixture, add the hydrated TVP, miso, breadcrumbs, and remaining seitan. Add salt and pepper to taste. Mix until well combined.

5. Shape the burgers. Heat a griddle over medium heat with a little sunflower oil, and cook the burgers until browned on both sides.

For the Japanese mayonnaise:

**½ cup soymilk
¾ cup sunflower oil
1 lime, for zest
1 teaspoon white miso
1 teaspoon vinegar
1 teaspoon Dijon mustard
1 tablespoon sugar**

1. In the bowl of a blender, add the soy milk and sunflower oil, and blend until emulsified.

2. Grate a little lime zest into the blender. Add the miso, vinegar, mustard, and sugar. Blend until creamy.

To assemble the burgers:

walnut rosemary buns (appendix) | Japanese mayonnaise | mint pickles (appendix) | marinated ginger | Japanese burgers | mint leaves, thinly sliced

1. Warm buns for 1 minute at 350°F.

2. On the bottom bun, spread a tablespoon of Japanese mayonnaise, then top with pickle slices, a few pieces of marinated ginger, the burgers, and finish with slices of mint. Add the top bun, and serve.

Smokey soy-nut burger
with chimichurri

To make the burgers:

⅓ cup walnuts | 1¾ cups TVP | water, or vegetable broth | 1 cucumber | 3 cloves garlic | 4 leaves of basil | ¼ teaspoon cumin | ½ teaspoon ras el hanout | 1 tablespoon smoked paprika | ¼ teaspoon nutmeg | 1 tablespoon toasted sesame seeds, ground | ½ cup breadcrumbs | olive oil | salt and pepper

1. Preheat oven to 350°F. Spread walnuts on baking sheet and toast until golden brown.

2. Soak TVP in water or vegetable broth until well hydrated. Strain to remove excess liquid.

3. In the bowl of a food processor, combine the hydrated TVP, toasted walnuts, cucumber, garlic, basil, cumin, ras el hanout, paprika, nutmeg, and sesame seeds. Blend well to combine. Transfer to a bowl.

4. To the seasoned mixture, add the breadcrumbs and 1 tablespoon of olive oil. Add salt and pepper to taste. Mix well to combine.

5. Shape the burgers. Heat a griddle over medium heat with a little olive oil and cook the burgers until browned on both sides.

For grilled vegetables:

1 zucchini, sliced | 1 onion, thinly sliced | olive oil | salt

1. On a griddle over medium-high heat, cook zucchini and onion with a little olive oil until golden browned.

2. Remove from heat and add salt to taste.

To assemble the burgers:

focaccia | chimichurri (appendix) | beefsteak tomato | smoky burgers | grilled vegetables

1. Cut the focaccia open and grill for a few seconds until toasted.

2. Spread chimichurri on the bottom slices, then top with tomato, burgers, and grilled vegetables. Serve hot.

White bean burger
with roasted cherry tomatoes

To make the burgers:

1¾ cups TVP
water, or vegetable broth
1 stick of celery
½ onion
2 cloves garlic
1 tablespoon Dijon mustard
¼ teaspoon ground cumin
1 lemon, for zest
½ cup canned white beans
½ cup breadcrumbs
olive oil
salt and pepper

1. Soak TVP in water or vegetable broth until well hydrated. Strain to remove excess liquid.

2. In the bowl of a food processor, combine celery, onion, garlic, mustard, cumin, lemon zest, and half of the beans. Blend until well combined. Transfer mixture to a bowl.

3. Add to this mixture the remaining beans, breadcrumbs and 2 tablespoons of olive oil. Add salt and pepper to taste. Mix well to combine.

4. Shape the burgers. Heat a griddle over medium heat with a little olive oil, and cook the burgers until browned on both sides.

For the roasted cherry tomatoes:

½ pint cherry tomatoes, halved
olive oil
salt

1. Preheat oven to 375°F.

2. Mix cherry tomatoes, olive oil, and salt to taste in a small bowl.

3. Spread tomatoes on baking sheet, and bake for 6–7 minutes.

To assemble the burgers:

crusty hamburger buns
bean burgers
roasted cherry tomatoes
arugula
rosemary-infused olive oil (appendix)
Maldon sea salt

1. Lightly toast the burger buns.

2. Place the burgers on the bottom buns and top with four cherry tomato halves, a few leaves of arugula, a drizzle of rosemary-infused olive oil, and a pinch of salt.

NOTE

Dijon is a yellow mustard with strong flavor.
It originates from Dijon, the city of the same
name, located about 180 miles from Paris.

Lebanese burger

To make the burgers:

½ onion
2 garlic cloves
¼ teaspoon cumin
¼ teaspoon cinnamon
1¼ tablespoons pine nuts
½ cup chopped parsley
1¾ cups cooked chickpeas
3 tablespoons breadcrumbs
salt and pepper
olive oil

1. In the bowl of a food processor, combine the onion, garlic, cumin, cinnamon, pine nuts, parsley, and 1 cup of chickpeas. Blend until well combined. Transfer mixture to a bowl.

2. To the chickpea mixture, add breadcrumbs and remaining chickpeas. Add salt and pepper to taste. Mix well to combine.

3. Shape the burgers. Heat a griddle over medium heat with a little olive oil, and cook the burgers until browned on both sides.

For the hummus with soy yogurt:

2 cups hummus (appendix)
1 tablespoon extra virgin olive oil
2 tablespoons unsweetened soy yogurt

1. Mix all ingredients in a bowl until well combined.

To assemble the burgers:

wheat tortillas
hummus with soy yogurt
sliced tomato
green lettuce
burgers

1. Warm the tortillas on a grill over high heat for a few seconds on both sides.

2. Top tortillas with 2 tablespoons of hummus with soy yogurt, sliced tomatoes, green lettuce, and burger patties. Wrap the tortilla around the filling.

Seitan burgers with roasted peppers
and raisin and pine nut spinach sauté

To make seitan burgers with roasted peppers:

2 red peppers | 1¼ tablespoons marcona almonds | 2 cloves garlic | ½ teaspoon Dijon mustard | 1¾ cup seitan (appendix) | ⅓ cup breadcrumbs | olive oil | salt and pepper

1. Preheat oven to 350°F. Put the peppers on a baking sheet, and roast for 30 minutes until skin is charred.

2. Spread almonds on another baking sheet, and bake until golden and toasted.

3. In the bowl of a food processor, add garlic, mustard, and seitan. Blend until well combined. Transfer mixture to a bowl.

4. Chop almonds. Peel peppers and remove seeds. Chop finely.

5. Add the chopped almonds, peppers, breadcrumbs, and 1 tablespoon of olive oil to the seitan mixture. Add salt and pepper to taste. Mix well to combine.

6. Shape the burgers. Heat a griddle over medium heat with a little olive oil, and cook the burgers until browned on both sides.

For raisin and pine nut spinach sauté:

1 tablespoon pine nuts | 4 cloves garlic, peeled and sliced | olive oil | 1 bunch fresh spinach | ¼ teaspoon nutmeg | 3 tablespoons raisins | salt

1. Toast the pine nuts in the oven at 350°F until slightly browned.

2. In a pan over medium heat, sauté garlic with 2 tablespoons of olive oil until fragrant.

3. Add the spinach and nutmeg. Sauté until spinach turns bright green. Add pine nuts, raisins, and salt to taste, and sauté for another minute.

To assemble the burgers:

ciabatta rolls | 4 tomatoes | olive oil | sea salt | burger with roasted peppers | raisin and pine nut spinach sauté

1. Cut the ciabatta rolls open, and toast at 350°F for a few seconds.

2. Cut the tomatoes in half, and rub over the toasted bread. Drizzle with olive oil and sea salt to taste.

3. Top the bread with burgers, and finish with raisin and pine nut spinach sauté.

Yellow curry burgers
with Thai coleslaw

To make the burgers:

2 cups TVP | water, or vegetable broth | 1 bunch cilantro | 1 lime, zested | 1 spring onion, chopped | 1 clove garlic | 2 tablespoons sour Thai sauce (appendix) | 1 tablespoon yellow curry paste | ⅓ cup breadcrumbs | salt and pepper | sunflower oil |

1. Soak TVP in water or vegetable broth until well hydrated. Strain to remove excess liquid.

2. In the bowl of a food processor, add cilantro, lime zest, spring onion, garlic clove, Thai sauce, yellow curry paste, and half the TVP. Blend until well combined. Transfer to a bowl.

3. To the curry mixture, add the remaining TVP, breadcrumbs, and salt and pepper to taste. Mix well to combine.

4. Shape the burgers. Heat a griddle over medium heat with a little sunflower oil, and cook the burgers until browned on both sides.

For the Thai coleslaw:

2 carrots, peeled into strips | ¼ napa cabbage, cored and sliced | 3 tablespoons mayonnaise (appendix) | 1 piece of ginger, peeled and grated | 1 spring onion, thinly sliced | juice of 2 limes | salt | pepper | basil leaves

1. In a large bowl, toss the carrots with the cabbage.

2. In a small bowl, mix the mayonnaise with the ginger, onion, and lime juice. Add to carrot mixture, and mix well. Add salt and pepper to taste, and toss with basil.

To assemble the burgers:

onion buns
yellow curry burgers
Thai coleslaw
basil leaves

1. Open the buns and toast in oven at 350°F for a few seconds.

2. Place a burger on each bun, and top generously with Thai coleslaw and basil leaves.

Black olive burgers
with peperonata

To make black olive burgers:

1¾ cups TVP | water, or vegetable broth | 2 cloves garlic | ½ cup chopped parsley | 2 cups pitted black olives | ½ cup breadcrumbs | salt | olive oil

1. Soak TVP in water or vegetable broth until well hydrated. Strain to remove excess liquid.

2. In the bowl of a food processor, combine garlic, parsley, olives, and half the hydrated TVP. Blend until well combined. Transfer mixture to a bowl.

3. To the olive mixture, add breadcrumbs, the rest of the hydrated TVP, and salt to taste. Mix until well combined.

4. Shape the burgers. Heat a griddle over medium heat with a little olive oil, and cook the burgers until browned on both sides.

For peperonata:

olive oil | 2 cloves garlic, chopped | 1 red onion, sliced | 2 red peppers | 1 cup crushed tomatoes | salt and pepper

1. In a skillet over medium heat, add 3 tablespoons of olive oil along with the garlic and onion. Cover the pan.

2. Meanwhile, remove seeds from red peppers, and slice thinly. Add to pan. Turn the heat to low and cook for 15 minutes.

3. Add the crushed tomatoes and cook another 15 minutes. Add salt and pepper to taste.

For grilled asparagus:

1 bunch asparagus | salt | oil

1. Toss the asparagus with salt and oil. Grill until bright green.

For fried tofu cubes:

one block soft tofu | soy sauce | vegetable oil

1. Cut the block of tofu into small cubes and marinate in soy sauce. Fry in vegetable or another neutral oil.

To assemble the burgers:

soft burger buns (appendix) | peperonata | grilled asparagus | black olive burgers | vegan cheese sauce (appendix) | fried tofu cubes | baked sweet potato strips (appendix)

1. Open the buns and toast them in the oven at 350°F for one minute.

2. On the bottom buns, top with peperonata, grilled asparagus, burgers, vegan cheese sauce, and a few cubes of fried tofu. Serve with baked sweet potato strips.

NOTE

Peperonata is a typical Sicilian dish made with peppers, tomatoes, onions, and garlic. It is usually served as a side dish or salad.

Falafel burgers
with caponata

To make falafel patties:

2 cups dried chickpeas | 2 cloves garlic | 1 onion | ½ cup chopped parsley | ½ cup chopped cilantro | 1 teaspoon cumin | 1 tablespoon breadcrumbs | salt and pepper | vegetable oil

1. Soak the chickpeas overnight (at least 10 hours). Strain.

2. In the bowl of a food processor, add chickpeas, garlic, onion, parsley, cilantro, cumin, and breadcrumbs. Blend until well combined. Transfer mixture to bowl. Add salt and pepper to taste.

3. Shape patties and fry in vegetable oil at 350°F.

For the caponata:

2 eggplants, sliced | salt | olive oil | 2 carrots, sliced | 1 red onion, sliced | ¼ stalk celery, diced | 4 green pitted olives, diced | 4 capers in salt | 2 tablespoons white wine vinegar | 1 tablespoon sugar

1. Toss eggplant with salt and set aside for 15 minutes.

2. In a nonstick skillet over medium heat, add enough olive oil to cover the bottom of the pan. Place the eggplant slices in the pan, topping with carrot, then onion, then the chopped celery, olives, and capers. Cover and cook over low heat for 30 minutes.

3. In a small saucepan over medium heat, combine the vinegar and sugar until boiling.

4. After vegetables have cooked for 30 minutes, add vinegar-sugar mixture, and cook for another 5 minutes. Turn off heat. Salt and pepper to taste.

To assemble the burgers:

bread | falafel burgers | caponata | extra virgin olive oil | basil leaves

1. Grill bread until toasted.

2. Top with falafel patties, caponata, a drizzle of olive oil, and basil leaves.

NOTE
Powdered smoke is a product that is used to give foods a slightly smoky flavor.

Beet burgers on pizzas

To make the beet burgers:

1 cup wheat semolina
3 cups vegetable broth
1⅓ cups cooked beets, grated
¼ cup chopped parsley
1 tablespoon smoked paprika
⅓ cup toasted hazelnuts
olive oil
salt and pepper to taste

1. In a small saucepan over low heat, combine the wheat semolina and vegetable broth and cover, cooking until the liquid has all been absorbed.

2. In the bowl of a food processor, add the cooked beets, parsley, smoked paprika, toasted hazelnuts, 1 tablespoon of olive oil, and half the semolina mixture. Blend until well combined. Transfer mixture to a bowl.

3. Stir in the remaining semolina, and add salt and pepper to taste.

4. Shape the burgers. Heat a griddle over medium heat with a little olive oil, and cook the burgers until browned on both sides.

For pizza:

2 cloves garlic, chopped
1 cup crushed tomatoes
pizza dough (appendix)

1. Preheat oven to 375°F.

2. In a small bowl, mix garlic and crushed tomatoes. Set aside.

3. Divide dough into 8 pieces, stretching each piece to have a 4-inch diameter. Spread tomato mixture onto each piece, and bake until the edges are browned. Remove from oven.

To assemble the burgers:

pizzas (appendix)
beet burgers
cherry tomatoes, quartered
arugula
Maldon sea salt
white truffle oil

1. Top each pizza with a burger. Garnish with cherry tomatoes, arugula, sea salt, and a drizzle of white truffle oil.

Falafel burgers
with tzatziki sauce

To make falafel patties:

2 cups dried chickpeas
2 garlic cloves
1 onion
½ cup chopped dill
zest of 1 lemon
1 teaspoon cumin
½ teaspoon dried rosemary
salt and pepper to taste
1 tablespoon breadcrumbs
vegetable oil

1. Soak the chickpeas overnight, or at least 10 hours. Strain.

2. In the bowl of a food processor, combine chickpeas, garlic, onion, dill, lemon zest, cumin, and rosemary. Blend until well combined. Transfer to a bowl. Add salt and pepper to taste.

3. Shape burgers. Fry in vegetable oil at 375°F.

For the tzatziki sauce:

1 cup natural unsweetened soy yogurt
1 cucumber, peeled and grated
1 clove garlic, chopped
juice of 1 lemon
¼ cup chopped dill
¼ cup chopped mint
extra virgin olive oil
salt and pepper

1. Combine all ingredients in a bowl. Add salt and pepper to taste. Store in the refrigerator.

To assemble the burgers:

soft burger buns (appendix)
tzatziki
falafel burgers
arugula

1. Cut open the bread and toast for 1 minute at 350°F.

2. Top the buns with chilled tzatziki and burgers. Garnish with arugula.

NOTE
Tzatziki is a classic sauce in Greek cuisine. It is also found in Turkish cooking. It is best served cold with pita bread.

Arancini burgers
stuffed with smoked tofu and saffron mayonnaise

To make arancini burgers:

3 cups water
1½ cups white rice
4 saffron strands
salt
2 tablespoons nutritional yeast
2 cloves garlic, chopped
1 onion, chopped
1 stalk celery, chopped
1 carrot, chopped
olive oil
½ cup crushed tomatoes
1 block smoked tofu, cut into small cubes
pepper
breadcrumbs
vegetable oil, for frying

1. In a small saucepan, bring water to a boil. Add the rice, saffron, and a pinch of salt. Cook until rice is very soft and water is absorbed. Add the yeast. Let cool in refrigerator.

2. In a pan over medium heat, combine garlic, onion, celery, carrot, and a little olive oil. Cover and cook for 10 minutes, stirring every 2 minutes.

3. Add crushed tomatoes and tofu to the pan and cook, covered, for 10 more minutes over low heat. Add salt and pepper to taste. Let the filling cool.

4. Take a handful of rice and pat into a bowl shape. Add a spoonful of tofu filling. Top with more rice. Form round burgers.

5. Brush burgers with a little water, and dip them in breadcrumbs, pressing well so they stick. Fry in oil at 375°F until golden brown.

For saffron mayonnaise:

5 strands saffron
2 cups mayonnaise (appendix)

1. Mix saffron into mayonnaise until well combined. The mayonnaise should be a bright yellow color.

To assemble the burgers:

soft burger buns (appendix)
tomato, sliced
spring onion, chopped
extra virgin olive oil
salt
arancini burgers
saffron mayonnaise

1. Toast the bread on both sides.

2. Top each slice with sliced tomatoes, spring onions, a splash of extra virgin olive oil, salt, a burger, and a dollop of saffron mayonnaise.

NOTE
Arancini, or rice croquettes, are very popular
in Sicilian cuisine. Saffron is responsible for
their characteristic yellow color.

Manchurian burgers

To make Manchurian burgers:

3 tablespoons cornstarch | **¼ cup water** | **4 carrots, peeled and grated** | **½ cabbage, cored and thinly sliced** | **3 tablespoons flour** | **2 tablespoons soy sauce** | **1 tablespoon sambal oelek (spicy chili sauce)** | **salt and pepper** | **vegetable oil, for frying**

1. In a small bowl, dilute the cornstarch with ¼ cup of water. Mix well.

2. In a medium bowl, toss the carrots and cabbage with the cornstarch mixture. Add the remaining ingredients (except salt, pepper, and vegetable oil), and mix well. Let rest 15 minutes. Add salt and pepper to taste.

3. Place mixture in the bowl of a food processor. Pulse until well combined.

4. Return mixture to the bowl, kneading by hand until a compact dough is formed.

5. Shape burgers. Fry in vegetable oil at 375°F until golden brown.

For the sauce:

sunflower oil | **8 cloves garlic, minced** | **1 onion, minced** | **1 piece of ginger, peeled and minced** | **4 mushrooms, sliced** | **1 tablespoon sugar** | **1 tablespoon soy sauce** | **1 tablespoon apple cider vinegar** | **1 tablespoon cornstarch, diluted in ¼ cup water** | **salt and pepper**

1. In a saucepan over low heat, warm 2 tablespoons of sunflower oil and sauté the garlic, onion, and ginger. Add the mushroom slices and cover. Cook for 10 minutes.

2. Add sugar, soy sauce, vinegar, cornstarch slurry, and salt and pepper to taste. Cook for 15 minutes over low heat. Transfer to blender or use an immersion blender. Blend until smooth.

For baked vegetables:

1 eggplant, coarsely chopped | **1 pepper, coarsely chopped** | **1 red onion, coarsely chopped** | **salt** **sunflower oil**

1. Preheat oven to 350°F.

2. Toss the chopped vegetables with salt and 2 tablespoons of sunflower oil.

3. Put vegetables into a baking dish, cover with foil and bake for 25 minutes.

To assemble the burgers:

soft burger buns (appendix) | **sauce** | **Manchurian burgers** | **baked vegetables** | **cilantro**

1. Cut the buns open and toast for 2 minutes at 350°F. Top bottom buns with 2 tablespoons of sauce. Top with burger, baked vegetables, and cilantro.

Lentil and rice burgers
with avocado and fennel

water | 1 cup white rice | 4 cloves garlic, peeled and minced | salt | 3¼ tablespoons pine nuts | 2 cups cooked lentils | 8 mint leaves, chopped | 2 tablespoons breadcrumbs | vegetable oil for frying | salt and pepper

1. Preheat oven to 375°F.

2. Bring a pot of water to boil. Add the rice, garlic, and salt. Cook until rice is very soft. Strain and transfer to fridge to cool.

3. Spread pine nuts on baking sheet, and toast in oven until golden. Let cool. Chop finely with a knife.

4. In a medium bowl, combine cold rice, cooked lentils, mint, pine nuts, breadcrumbs, and salt and pepper to taste.

5. Shape the burgers. Brush burgers with a little water and dip in breadcrumbs, pressing to help them stick. Fry at 375°F until golden brown.

For the marinated fennel:

1 fennel bulb, trimmed and thinly sliced | juice of 1 lemon | extra virgin olive oil | salt

1. In a medium bowl, combine fennel slices, lemon juice, 2 tablespoons of extra virgin olive oil, and salt. Let marinate in the fridge for a few hours.

To assemble the burgers:

whole grain rolls (appendix)
1 carrot
2 avocados
marinated fennel
lentil and rice burgers
paprika
extra virgin olive oil
sea salt

1. Toast the bread in the oven at 350°F for 2 minutes. Peel the carrot and cut strips using the peeler.

2. Open the avocados and remove the pit. Slice lengthwise and scoop out the flesh with a spoon.

3. Top the toast with marinated fennel, carrot ribbons, burgers, a few slices of avocado, paprika, a drizzle of olive oil, and a sprinkle of sea salt.

Smoked tofu sandwich
with sprouts and tofu mayonnaise

For the smoked tofu:

2 smoked tofu blocks
1 head of garlic
1 piece of ginger, coarsely chopped
1½ cups soy sauce
1½ cups water
1 sprig of rosemary

1. Cut the tofu into four thin, wide steaks. Cut the head of garlic in half.

2. To make the marinade, combine garlic, ginger, soy sauce, water, and rosemary.

3. Place the tofu steaks in a container and pour marinade over top. Cover and leave in refrigerator at least 12 hours.

4. On a griddle over high heat, grill the tofu steaks until well marked.

To make tofu mayonnaise:

½ cup raw macadamia nuts
water
2 cups soft tofu
juice of 1 lemon
salt

1. Soak macadamia nuts for 24 hours, changing water every 8 hours.

2. In the bowl of a blender, combine tofu, hydrated macadamia nuts, lemon juice, and pinch of salt. Blend until creamy. Add water, a tablespoon at a time, if necessary.

To assemble the burgers:

1 carrot
rye bread
tofu mayonnaise
scallions, thinly sliced
smoked tofu
beefsteak tomato, sliced
salt

1. Peel the carrots into strips using a peeler.

2. Top each piece of bread with a spoonful of tofu mayonnaise, scallion, slices of smoked tofu, one or two slices of tomato, and carrot ribbons. Sprinkle salt to taste.

> **NOTE**
> The beefsteak tomato gets its name because of its size and color. One tomato can grow to weigh up to 2 pounds. They are juicy with thin, tender skin.

Grilled seitan sandwiches
with butternut squash and light mayonnaise

For seitan steaks:

3 cups water
1 tablespoon soy sauce
zest and juice of 1 orange
1 onion, peeled and quartered
2 sprigs thyme
2 blocks seitan

1. To make marinade, combine water, soy sauce, orange zest, orange juice, onion, and thyme.

2. Cut the seitan into 8 steaks. Place the steaks in a container and pour marinade over them. Cover and store in refrigerator for at least 12 hours.

3. On a griddle over high heat, grill marinated seitan steaks on both sides until well browned.

For butternut squash:

1 butternut squash, peeled and thinly sliced
1 tablespoon olive oil
salt

1. In a covered pan over low heat, cook squash slices for 15 minutes with olive oil and salt.

To assemble the burgers:

seeded spelt bread
lettuce
butternut squash
seitan steaks
three small cucumbers, sliced lengthwise
light mayonnaise (appendix)
baked sweet potato strips (appendix)

1. Top bread slices with lettuce leaves, butternut squash, grilled seitan steaks, more butternut squash, cucumber slices, and a dollop of light mayonnaise.

2. Serve with baked sweet potato strips.

"Mean Mr. Mustard" burgers
with red wine shallots

For "Mean Mr. Mustard" burgers:

2 cups Mediterranean bites from Divina Teresa
1 clove garlic
handful fresh parsley
¼ teaspoon nutmeg
1 tablespoon mustard
salt and pepper
water
2 tablespoons breadcrumbs
panko
sunflower oil

1. In the bowl of a food processor, combine the Divina Teresa bites, garlic, parsley, nutmeg, and mustard. Blend until well combined. Transfer mixture to a bowl. Add 2 tablespoons of breadcrumbs and salt and pepper to taste, and mix well.

2. Shape the burgers. Brush with a little water and dip in panko, pressing to help it stick. Fry in sunflower oil at 375°F for 2 minutes.

For red wine shallots:

8 shallots, peeled and sliced
1 tablespoon olive oil
2 cups red wine
½ cup water
1 tablespoon sugar
salt

1. In a skillet over medium heat, cook the shallots in olive oil until lightly browned.

2. Add the wine, water, sugar, and salt to taste. Cover and cook over low heat until liquid reduces to only one-fourth of its previous volume.

To assemble the burgers:

Galician bread
"Mean Mr. Mustard" burgers
mayonnaise (appendix)
shallots in red wine
sage leaves
freshly ground pepper

1. Slice the bread and toast in the oven at 350°F for 1 minute.

2. Place burgers on buns, topping with mayonnaise, shallots, sage, and freshly ground pepper.

> **NOTE**
>
> Divina Teresa is a company that makes vegan food products. Panko is a type of coarse breadcrumbs. It is widely used in Japan to coat foods for frying.

Leek and peanut burgers
with cashew cheese

For leek burgers:

1 leek
1 tablespoon olive oil
1¼ cups cava (sparkling wine)
4 cups Atlantic bites from Divine Teresa
1 tablespoon peanut butter
1½ tablespoons breadcrumbs
salt and pepper | sunflower oil

1. Trim the leek. Slice open lengthwise and rinse thoroughly to remove any dirt. Slice thinly.

2. In a pan over medium heat, cook the leeks with 1 tablespoon of olive oil for 4 minutes.

3. Add the cava and continue cooking, stirring occasionally to prevent sticking. Cook for 5 more minutes until the cava has reduced.

4. In the bowl of a food processor, combine Atlantic bites, cooked leeks, and peanut butter. Blend until well combined. Transfer to a bowl.

5. Add breadcrumbs and salt and pepper to taste, and knead until well combined.

6. Shape burgers. Fry in sunflower oil at 350°F for 2 minutes.

For cashew cheese:

2 cups vegan cheese (appendix)
1 cup water

1. Mix the cheese with the water until well combined.

For grilled eggplant:

1 eggplant, sliced in ½ inch–thick half-moons
salt | olive oil

1. Toss eggplant slices with salt, and leave in colander for 10 minutes.

2. In a skillet over medium heat, cook eggplant slices with 1 tablespoon of olive oil.

To assemble the burgers:

country bread
extra virgin olive oil
leek burgers
cashew cheese
grilled eggplant
fresh spinach
patatas bravas (appendix)

1. Cut the country bread into slices and toast at 350°F for 2 minutes. Drizzle with extra virgin olive oil.

2. Top each slice with burger patty and a dollop of cashew cheese. Add a few slices of eggplant, and top with fresh spinach. Serve with *patatas bravas*.

Sage millet burgers
with butternut squash and roasted artichokes

For millet burgers:

1 butternut squash, peeled, seeded, and cubed
water
4 capers in salt, rinsed
10 sage leaves
1 cup millet
salt
olive oil

1. Preheat oven to 375°F. Spread squash cubes in a baking pan and cover with foil. Bake until tender.

2. In the bowl of a food processor, combine the roasted squash, 3 cups water, capers, and sage leaves. Blend until smooth.

3. In a saucepan, combine millet, salt, and the squash mixture. Cook over low heat until liquid has cooked off and mixture is thick. Remove from heat and let cool.

4. Shape burgers. Place on baking tray. Brush with olive oil, and bake at 350°F for 10 minutes.

To assemble the burgers:

soft burger buns (appendix)
chipotle BBQ sauce (appendix)
millet burgers
lettuce
mayonnaise (appendix)
cayenne
Tofutti cream cheese
roasted artichokes (appendix)
thick-cut fries (appendix)

1. Toast burger buns on both sides until golden brown.

2. Top each bun with chipotle BBQ sauce, a burger, a few leaves of lettuce, tablespoon of mayonnaise, a pinch of cayenne, a little cream cheese, and roasted artichokes. Serve with thick-cut fries.

NOTE
Tofutti cream cheese is made from water, vegetable fats, and tofu.

Pea and mint burgers
with sprouts

To make the burgers:

1¼ cups TVP
water, or vegetable broth
1 cup seitan (appendix)
15 mint leaves
2 cloves garlic
⅓ cup breadcrumbs
½ cup fresh peas
olive oil
salt and pepper

1. Soak TVP in water or vegetable broth until well hydrated. Strain to remove excess liquid.

2. In the bowl of a food processor, combine the seitan, mint leaves, garlic, and half the hydrated TVP. Blend until well combined. Transfer mixture to a bowl.

3. To this mixture, add breadcrumbs, peas, 1 tablespoon of olive oil, salt and pepper to taste, and the remaining TVP. Mix well to combine.

4. Shape burgers. Brush them with a little olive oil, place on a cookie sheet, and bake at 350°F for 10 minutes.

To assemble the burgers:

hamburger buns (appendix)
Dijon mustard
fennel
avocado
pea and mint burgers
sprouts
Thai sweet and sour sauce (appendix)

1. Toast the hamburger buns in the oven at 350°F for 30 seconds. Spread Dijon mustard on top of the bread.

2. Cut the fennel with a mandolin into thin strips. Open the avocado in half and remove strips with a knife.

3. Top each roll with fennel slices, a burger, sprouts, and avocado slices. Top with Thai sweet and sour sauce.

Seitan sandwich
with asparagus and cheddar-style cheese

To make seitan steaks with asparagus:

water
2 bunches of asparagus, stemmed
16 seitan steaks (appendix)
8 mushrooms, stemmed and halved
olive oil
salt and pepper

1. Bring a saucepan of water to boil over high heat. Add the asparagus and cook it for 1 minute. Drain asparagus and plunge into cold water to stop cooking.

2. On a griddle over medium heat, cook the seitan, asparagus, and mushrooms in a little olive oil until browned on all sides. Sprinkle with salt and pepper to taste.

For cheddar-style cheese:

½ yellow pepper, stem and seeds removed
¼ spring onion, sliced (white parts only)
½ cup raw cashews
6 tablespoons water
1 tablespoon nutritional yeast
1 tablespoon tahini
¼ clove garlic
1 teaspoon salt

1. In the bowl of a food processor, combine all ingredients. Blend until smooth.

For the tomato brunoise:

water
1 pound of tomatoes

1. Bring a pot of water to a boil. Make a small cut in the bottom of each tomato. Drop tomatoes gently into boiling water for 10 seconds. Remove and plunge into cold water to stop cooking.

2. Peel and quarter tomatoes, and remove the seeds. Cut tomatoes into ½-inch cubes.

To assemble the burgers:

seeded bread
mayonnaise (appendix)
seitan steaks
cheddar sauce
asparagus
mushrooms, cut in halves
tomato brunoise
thick-cut fries (appendix)

1. Slice the bread. Spread mayonnaise on each slice. On each bun, place a seitan steak, a spoonful of cheddar sauce, 4 asparagus spears, another seitan steak, and another spoonful of cheddar sauce.

2. Top with mushroom halves and tomato brunoise. Serve with thick-cut fries.

Spinach-polenta burgers
with artichoke chips

For spinach-polenta burgers:

2½ cups vegetable broth
1 bunch spinach
3 tablespoons olive oil
¾ cup quick-cooking polenta
salt and pepper

1. In a saucepan over medium heat, bring the vegetable broth and spinach to a boil. Turn heat to low and cook for 2 minutes.

2. Add the olive oil and the quick-cooking polenta, and stir vigorously over low heat until fully cooked. Add salt and pepper to taste.

3. Transfer to a bowl or container, and cover with plastic wrap. Let mixture cool to room temperature.

4. Shape burgers. Bake at 350°F for 5 minutes.

For artichoke chips:

2 artichokes
sunflower oil
juice of 1 lemon
1 sprig of thyme, stemmed
sea salt

1. Cut the stem off the artichokes. Remove the tough outer leaves. Cut in half and slice thinly.

2. Fry slices in sunflower oil at 350°F until golden.

3. Transfer to a plate lined with paper towels to absorb oil.

4. Toss chips with lemon juice, thyme leaves, and sea salt.

To assemble the burgers:

rye bread
aioli (appendix)
spinach-polenta burgers
beefsteak tomato, sliced
artichoke chips
green lettuce

1. Top each slice of bread with a spoonful of aioli, a burger, a few slices of tomato, artichoke chips, and a few leaves of lettuce.

Vaskintops

To make seitan burgers and herbs:

2 cups seitan | 3 tablespoons pine nuts | 4 cloves roasted garlic (appendix) | 1 bunch fresh cilantro | 4 sage leaves | 12 basil leaves | ½ teaspoon smoked paprika | 1 tablespoon prepared mustard | ½ teaspoon oregano | 1¼ tablespoons bread-crumbs | salt and pepper | olive oil

1. In the bowl of a food processor, combine seitan, pine nuts, garlic, cilantro, sage, basil, smoked paprika, mustard, and oregano. Blend until well combined. Transfer mixture to a bowl.

2. Add the breadcrumbs and salt and pepper to taste. Mix well to combine.

3. Shape the burgers. Heat a griddle over medium heat with a little olive oil and cook the burgers until browned on both sides.

For yellow pepper sauce:

2 yellow peppers | 2 cloves garlic | extra virgin olive oil | salt

1. Preheat oven to 350°F. Remove stems and seeds from peppers. Place peppers in a baking dish, and roast for 25 minutes.

2. Let them cool. Remove skins and place peppers in the bowl of a food processor with garlic, olive oil, and salt to taste. Blend until smooth.

For shiitakes with lemon:

16 shiitakes, halved | juice of 1 lemon | olive oil | salt

1. Toss shiitakes with lemon juice and marinate for 15 minutes.

2. In a skillet over high heat, sauté shiitakes with olive oil until golden. Add salt to taste.

For tomato toast:

bread | 4 tomatoes, halved | extra virgin olive oil | sea salt

1. Thinly slice the bread and toast for 4 minutes at 350°F.

2. Rub halved tomatoes on toast. Drizzle with olive oil and sea salt.

To assemble the burgers:

tomato toast | yellow pepper sauce | seitan burgers | shiitakes with lemon | basil leaves | mustard | BBQ sauce (appendix)

1. Top toast with yellow pepper sauce. Layer burgers, shiitakes, basil leaves, and top with another slice of tomato toast.

2. Serve with a few spoonfuls of mustard and BBQ sauce on the side.

Spicy lentil and millet burgers
with tartar sauce

To make lentil and millet burgers:

2½ cups vegetable broth
¾ cup millet
1 cup cooked lentils
1 tablespoon sriracha
½ cup toasted hazelnuts, ground
½ teaspoon smoked paprika
salt
olive oil

1. In a saucepan, combine vegetable broth and millet. Cook over low heat until the liquid is evaporated and millet is cooked. Transfer to a bowl.

2. To the cooked millet, add the cooked lentils, sriracha, toasted hazelnut flour, paprika, and salt to taste. Mix until well combined.

3. Shape the burgers. Heat a griddle over medium heat with a generous pour of olive oil and cook the burgers until browned on both sides.

To assemble the burgers:

soft burger buns (appendix)
BBQ sauce (appendix)
spicy lentil and millet burgers
tartar sauce (appendix)
sliced tomato
watercress
extra virgin olive oil flavored with pepper (optional)

1. Toast bread. Top with BBQ sauce and a burger. Brush burger with more BBQ sauce. Top with a dollop of tartar sauce, sliced tomatoes, watercress, and a little spicy olive oil.

NOTE
Sriracha is a spicy Asian sauce used to flavor dishes. It is made from chiles and garlic.

Quinoa, lentil, and dill burgers
with sun-dried tomato pesto

To make burgers:

2 cups mushroom broth (appendix)
1 cup quinoa
½ cup chopped fresh dill
½ cup chopped arugula
½ teaspoon cilantro
1¼ tablespoons oats
salt and pepper | 2 cups cooked lentils

1. In a small saucepan, combine the mushroom broth and quinoa, and cook, covered, over low heat until the quinoa has absorbed all the broth, approximately 15 minutes.

2. In the bowl of a food processor, combine quinoa, dill, arugula, cilantro, oats, and salt and pepper to taste. Blend until well combined. Transfer to a bowl.

3. Add lentils and mash with a fork until well combined. Let stand 15 minutes at room temperature, covered with plastic wrap to keep moist.

4. Shape burgers. In a nonstick pan over medium heat, cook burgers on both sides until browned.

For sun-dried tomato sauce:

2 cups sun-dried tomatoes in oil | 3 tomatoes | 1 red onion | 2 tablespoons raisins, or dried currants | juice of 1 lemon | ½ tablespoon thyme | ½ teaspoon salt

1. In the bowl of a food processor, combine all ingredients. Blend until smooth.

For marinated vegetables:

1 avocado, diced
1 yellow pepper, diced
1 red onion, diced
1 teaspoon apple cider vinegar
1 tablespoon olive oil
¼ teaspoon salt

1. In a bowl, combine all ingredients. Let sit at room temperature.

To assemble the burgers:

seeded hamburger buns
sun-dried tomato sauce
lentil burgers | marinated vegetables

1. Toast the bread in the oven at 350°F. Top with sun-dried tomato sauce and burgers, and garnish with marinated vegetables.

Heavy metal burger

For burgers:

2 red peppers, stemmed and seeded
2 cups vegetable broth
½ cup millet
1 cup cooked chickpeas
½ teaspoon coriander
¼ teaspoon nutmeg
1 tablespoon mustard
1 tablespoon nutritional yeast
3 tablespoons oats
salt and pepper | olive oil

1. Preheat oven to 350°F. Place peppers on tray and roast for 25 minutes, until skin is blistered. Set aside.

2. Once cool enough to handle, peel peppers and place in bowl of a food processor. Add vegetable broth and blend until smooth.

3. In a saucepan, combine millet and pepper puree, and cook over low heat for 15 minutes, until millet has absorbed the liquid.

4. Mash chickpeas, coriander, and nutmeg with a mortar and pestle, then transfer mixture to a bowl. Add the cooked millet, mustard, nutritional yeast, and oats. Add salt and pepper to taste. Let mixture stand for 15 minutes until oats are well-hydrated.

5. Shape burgers. Cook in skillet with plenty of olive oil until well-browned.

To make the roasted beets:

3 raw beets, peeled and sliced
2 tablespoons olive oil
1 clove garlic, chopped
½ teaspoon salt

1. Preheat oven to 350°F. Line baking sheet with foil.

2. In a bowl, toss beet slices, olive oil, garlic, and salt.

3. Spread beets on prepared baking sheet and roast for 30 minutes.

To assemble the burgers:

hamburger buns (appendix)
roasted beets
mayonnaise (appendix)
heavy metal burgers
arugula

1. Toast the bread in the oven at 350°F for 1 minute. Top bread with two or three slices of beet. Add a tablespoon of mayonnaise, burger, and garnish with plenty of arugula.

Black rice burgers
with asparagus, mushrooms, and mustard vinaigrette

To make black rice burgers:

water
1 cup black rice
1 red onion
8 ounces tofu
3 tablespoons tomato paste
2 tablespoons breadcrumbs
salt and pepper | olive oil

1. Bring water to boil in a pot. Add black rice and cook for 6 minutes. Strain and let cool.

2. Grate the onion and tofu in a bowl. Add the black rice, tomato paste, breadcrumbs, and salt and pepper to taste. Mix well.

3. Shape the burgers. Heat a griddle over medium heat with a little olive oil, and cook the burgers until browned on both sides.

For asparagus and mushrooms:

water
1 bunch asparagus, thinly sliced lengthwise
½ cup bunashimeji (brown beech mushrooms), stemmed and sliced
2 tablespoons olive oil | salt

1. In a saucepan over high heat, bring water to a boil. Quickly blanch the asparagus for 20 seconds. Remove from water and plunge into cold water to stop cooking.

2. In a skillet over high heat, sauté mushrooms, asparagus, and olive oil for one minute. Remove from heat, and add a pinch of salt.

For mustard vinaigrette:

4 tablespoons white wine vinegar
2 tablespoons olive oil
1 tablespoon agave syrup
1 tablespoon Dijon mustard
½ teaspoon salt

1. Mix all ingredients together in a bowl. Reserve vinaigrette at room temperature.

To assemble the burgers:

English muffins
sour cream (appendix)
black rice burgers
asparagus and mushrooms
mustard vinaigrette

1. Toast muffins on a griddle over high heat for a few seconds or until golden.

2. On the bottom half of the muffin, add a dollop of sour cream, a black rice burger, and top with sautéed asparagus and mushrooms. Top with mustard vinaigrette.

Black rice and quinoa burgers

To make black rice and quinoa burgers:

water
1¼ tablespoons black rice
8 ounces tofu, mashed
2 cloves garlic, minced
½ cup quinoa
2 cups mushroom broth (appendix)
½ cup chopped fresh dill
salt and pepper | breadcrumbs | olive oil

1. Bring a small pot of water to a boil. Add the black rice and cook for 6 minutes. Strain and let cool. Combine with tofu and garlic.

2. In a small saucepan, combine quinoa and mushroom broth. Cook, covered, over medium heat until the broth is absorbed—about 15 minutes once the liquid begins to boil.

3. In a bowl, combine black rice, quinoa, dill, and salt and pepper to taste. Little by little, add enough breadcrumbs to make the mixture hold together.

4. Shape the burgers. Heat a griddle over medium heat with a little olive oil, and cook the burgers until browned on both sides.

For the balsamic onions:

5 tablespoons balsamic vinegar
3 tablespoons agave syrup
2 red onions, thinly sliced | olive oil

1. Mix vinegar with agave syrup.

2. In a skillet over medium heat, sear onions with a little olive oil. Pour balsamic mixture over onions and cook until liquid evaporates.

For the cucumber and tomato salad:

1 tomato, chopped
1 cucumber, chopped
¼ bunch parsley, chopped
juice of 2 lemons
2 tablespoons extra virgin olive oil
½ teaspoon salt

1. Combine all ingredients in a bowl. Let sit at room temperature.

To assemble the burgers:

English muffins
balsamic onions
black rice and quinoa burgers
cucumber and tomato salad
ketchup (appendix)

1. Toast muffins on a griddle over high heat until well marked.

2. Top muffins with balsamic onions, burger patties, and two spoonfuls of cucumber and tomato salad. Spread the top of the muffins with a little ketchup.

White bean burgers
with ginger and cilantro

To make burgers:

4 cups white beans, mashed
½ cup chopped fresh cilantro
1½ tablespoons grated fresh ginger or
1 teaspoon dried ground ginger
1½ teaspoons turmeric
⅓ cup breadcrumbs
salt and pepper to taste
olive oil

1. Combine all ingredients (except olive oil) in a bowl.

2. Shape the burgers. Heat a griddle over medium heat with a little olive oil, and cook the burgers until browned on both sides.

For seasoned broccoli:

1 bunch broccoli
water
1 red onion, diced
2 tablespoons olive oil
½ teaspoon ground cumin
½ teaspoon ground coriander
¼ teaspoon cinnamon
salt

1. Trim the broccoli into florets. Bring a pot of water to a boil. Add broccoli and cook for 2 minutes. Strain and immerse immediately in cold water.

2. In a skillet over medium heat, cook onion in olive oil for 1 minute. Add spices.

3. Add broccoli, and sauté for 2 minutes. Season with salt to taste.

To assemble the burgers:

seeded hamburger buns
baba ganoush (appendix)
white bean burgers
seasoned broccoli

1. Toast the buns on a griddle over high heat until well marked.

2. Top the bottom buns with baba ganoush, a burger patty, and plenty of seasoned broccoli.

Teriyaki burgers
with grilled pineapple

To make teriyaki burgers:

½ cup quinoa
1 cup vegetable broth (appendix)
1½ cups seitan (appendix)
3 tablespoons teriyaki sauce (appendix)
1¼ tablespoons oats
olive oil

1. In a saucepan over low heat, combine quinoa and broth. Cover and cook until quinoa has boiled for about 15 minutes and absorbed all the broth.

2. In the bowl of a food processor, combine cooked quiona, seitan, teriyaki sauce, and oats. Blend until well combined. Transfer mixture to a bowl.

3. Form burgers. Brush with olive oil, and bake on baking sheet at 350°F for 10 minutes.

For grilled pineapple:

¼ pineapple

1. Peel and slice the pineapple into triangles, to match the size of the burger bun.

2. On a griddle over high heat, cook the pineapple until well marked.

To assemble the burgers:

seeded burger buns
mustard
tomatoes, sliced
teriyaki burgers
grilled pineapple
green lettuce
apricot ketchup (appendix)

1. Toast the rolls in the oven at 350°F for 1 minute.

2. On the bottom bun, spread a little mustard. Top with tomato slices, teriyaki burgers, a triangle of grilled pineapple, and a leaf of lettuce. Brush the top bun with a little apricot ketchup.

Bulgur and roasted garlic burgers
with coleslaw

For bulgur and roasted garlic burgers:

2 cups vegetable broth
1 cup bulgur
1 head of roasted garlic (appendix)
¼ cup fresh parsley
½ cup toasted walnuts, chopped
1 tablespoon paprika
2 tablespoons breadcrumbs
salt and pepper
sunflower oil

1. In a small saucepan over medium heat, combine vegetable broth and bulgur. Cover and cook for about 20 minutes or until the bulgur has absorbed all the broth.

2. Mash roasted garlic, parsley, and toasted walnuts with a mortar and pestle.

3. In a medium bowl, mix the cooked bulgur, garlic-parsley-nut mixture, paprika, and breadcrumbs, and salt and pepper to taste.

4. Form the mixture into burger patties. Fry in sunflower oil over medium heat until golden on both sides.

For the coleslaw:

2 carrots, grated
¼ cabbage, grated
1 apple, cubed
1 spring onion, thinly sliced
1 cup unsweetened soy yogurt
2 tablespoons vinegar
1 teaspoon mustard
1 cucumber, thinly sliced
zest of 1 lime
salt and pepper

1. Combine all ingredients in a bowl and mix until well combined.

To assemble the burgers:

mustard
seeded burger buns
tomato slices
bulgur and roasted garlic burger
coleslaw
green lettuce

1. Spread some mustard on the bottom of each bun. Top with a slice of tomato, a burger patty, 2 tablespoons of coleslaw, and some lettuce leaves.

Catalan burgers

For Catalan burgers:

3 red peppers, roughly chopped
1 onion, roughly chopped
4 cups seitan (appendix)
2 cups smoked tofu
1½ tablespoons nutritional yeast
1½ tablespoons smoked paprika
⅓ cup breadcrumbs
½ teaspoon powdered smoke
salt and pepper
olive oil

1. Preheat oven to 350°F.

2. Wrap peppers and onion in foil and bake for 30 minutes.

3. In the bowl of a food processor, combine seitan, smoked tofu, roasted peppers and onions, nutritional yeast, smoked paprika, breadcrumbs, and powdered smoke. Add salt and pepper to taste. Blend until well combined. Transfer to a bowl. Let stand for 5 minutes to allow the breadcrumbs to absorb the moisture.

4. Form the burgers. Heat a griddle over medium heat with a little olive oil, and cook the burgers until browned on both sides.

To make the Romesco sauce:

5 ripe tomatoes
5 cloves garlic
1 slice of bread
1¼ tablespoons toasted hazelnuts
1 tablespoon vinegar
2 tablespoons olive oil
salt

1. Place the tomatoes and garlic in a pan, and bake at 350°F for 20 minutes.

2. Remove the pan from the oven and let cool. Peel the tomatoes and garlic.

3. Toast the slice of bread for 5 minutes at 350°F. In the bowl of a food processor, combine toasted bread, toasted hazelnuts, tomatoes, garlic, vinegar, olive oil, and a pinch of salt. Blend until smooth.

To assemble the burgers:

seeded burger buns
tomato, sliced
catalan burgers
Romesco sauce
fresh spinach

1. Toast the burger buns. Top with sliced tomato, burger, a tablespoon of Romesco sauce, and spinach leaves.

Ulysses burgers

3 tablespoons quinoa
½ cup vegetable broth
1¾ cups TVP
water, or vegetable broth
½ cup pine nuts
1 tablespoon ketchup (appendix)
1 cup cooked lentils
1 tablespoon Dijon mustard
2 tablespoons vegan Worcestershire sauce
    (appendix)
2 cloves garlic
¼ cup chopped fresh chives
¼ cup chopped fresh cilantro
⅓ cup breadcrumbs
salt and pepper
olive oil

1. In a small saucepan, combine quinoa and ½ cup vegetable broth. Simmer covered for 15 minutes until quinoa has absorbed all the broth.

2. Soak TVP in water or vegetable broth until well hydrated. Strain to remove excess liquid.

3. In the bowl of a food processor, combine hydrated TVP, cooked quinoa, pine nuts, ketchup, mustard, vegan Worcestershire sauce, garlic, chives, cilantro, and breadcrumbs. Blend until well combined. Add salt and pepper to taste. Transfer to bowl. Let rest for 10 minutes until breadcrumbs absorb all moisture.

4. Shape the burgers. Heat a griddle over medium heat with a little olive oil, and cook the burgers until browned on both sides.

To make the caramelized onions, Ulysses-style:

3 red onions, thinly sliced
2 tablespoons olive oil
3 tablespoons molasses

1. In a skillet over medium heat, sauté the onion in olive oil for 2 minutes. Add molasses and cook, covered, for 5 minutes.

To assemble the burgers:

soft burger buns (appendix)
tartar sauce (appendix)
soy burgers
caramelized onions
sea salt
french fries (appendix)

1. Toast bread well. Top with a tablespoon of tartar sauce, a burger patty, 2 tablespoons of caramelized onions, and sea salt. Serve with fries.

Vegan schnitzel
with mustard-basil vinaigrette

To make the schnitzel:

zest of 1 lemon
1¼ tablespoons breadcrumbs
1 tablespoon nutritional yeast
1 clove garlic
2 tablespoons chopped fresh parsley
salt and pepper
1¾ cups seitan (appendix)
water | crispy breadcrumbs
sunflower oil

1. In the bowl of a food processor, combine lemon zest, breadcrumbs, nutritional yeast, garlic, parsley, and salt and pepper to taste. Blend until well combined.

2. Shape schnitzel, and let stand for 10 minutes at room temperature.

3. Brush schnitzels with water and dip in crispy breadcrumbs, pressing to help them stick. Fry in sunflower oil at 350°F until golden, turning if necessary.

For mustard-basil vinaigrette:

4 tablespoons white wine vinegar
2 tablespoons olive oil
1 tablespoon agave syrup
1 tablespoon Dijon mustard
½ teaspoon salt | 8 basil leaves, sliced

1. Mix all ingredients together in a bowl. Set aside at room temperature.

To assemble the burgers:

1 cucumber
walnut rosemary buns (appendix)
aioli (appendix)
vegan cheddar cheese (appendix)
schnitzel
tomato, sliced
mustard-basil vinaigrette

1. Peel cucumber into thin strips.

2. Toast bread at 350°F for 2 minutes.

3. Spread aioli on the toast and top with vegan cheddar cheese, schnitzel, tomato slices, cucumber strips, and mustard-basil vinaigrette.

NOTE
The schnitzel have a similar texture to that of cooked scallops.

Mock-chicken burgers
with red cabbage salad

To make burgers:

2 cups diced vegetable product from Vegesan
½ tablespoon brown sugar
¼ teaspoon ground ginger
salt and pepper
1¼ tablespoons breadcrumbs
water
panko
sunflower oil

1. In the bowl of a food processor, combine diced vegetable product, brown sugar, ginger, and salt and pepper to taste. Blend until well combined. Transfer to a bowl. Add breadcrumbs and knead to mix well.

2. Shape the burger. Brush with a little water and dip in panko.

3. Fry them in sunflower oil at 350–375°F for 2 minutes.

For red cabbage salad:

¼ red cabbage, shredded
⅛ napa cabbage, shredded
1 spring onion, thinly sliced
2 tablespoons raisins, chopped
1 cup mayonnaise (appendix)
zest and juice of 1 lemon
salt

1. Combine all ingredients in a bowl and mix well.

To assemble the burgers:

soft burger buns (appendix)
dill mustard (appendix)
red lettuce
mock-chicken burgers
red cabbage salad

1. Toast the bread in the oven at 350°F for 30 seconds.

2. Top the bottom of each bun with dill mustard, a few leaves of red lettuce, a burger patty, and 2 tablespoons of red cabbage salad.

The skyscraper

To make red lentil burgers:

1¾ cups red lentils
1 carrot
1 red onion
½ teaspoon ground cumin
1 tablespoon nutritional yeast
¼ cup chopped fresh cilantro
1 tablespoon sambal oelek (spicy chili sauce)
1¼ tablespoons breadcrumbs
salt
olive oil

1. Bring a small pot of water to boil on the stove and cook the red lentils 5-6 minutes. Drain.

2. In the bowl of a food processor, combine the carrot and onion and blend until finely chopped.

3. In a medium bowl, mix the cooked lentils, cumin, nutritional yeast, carrot mixture, cilantro, samba oelek, breadcrumbs, and salt to taste. Mix until well combined.

4. Shape burgers. Place patties on baking tray and brush with olive oil. Bake at 350°F for 15 minutes or until golden brown.

For grilled eggplant:

salt
1 eggplant, sliced
3 tablespoons soy sauce
juice of 1 orange

1. Salt eggplant and leave in a strainer while you prepare the marinade.

2. In a small bowl, combine the soy sauce and orange juice. Move eggplant to a shallow bowl. Pour marinade over the eggplant, and let sit for 15 minutes.

3. On a griddle over medium heat, cook eggplants until they are browned.

To assemble the burgers:

soft burger buns (appendix)
strawberry BBQ sauce (appendix)
sliced tomato
grilled eggplant
red lentil burgers
vegan cheddar cheese
arugula
sour cream (appendix)

1. Toast the bread in the oven at 350°F for 1 minute.

2. Spread some strawberry BBQ sauce on each piece of toast. Place 2 slices of tomato, 2 slices of grilled eggplant, a burger patty, a slice of cheddar cheese, another burger patty, another slice of cheddar cheese, arugula, and a dollop of sour cream.

Delicious burgers
with eggplant caviar

To make burgers:

water | 1 cup black rice | 1 potato, cubed | 1 carrot, grated | ¼ teaspoon ground coriander | 2 tablespoons tomato paste | 1 tablespoon nutritional yeast | 4 tablespoons oats | salt | panko | sunflower oil

1. Bring a pot of water to a boil. Stir in the rice, cooking until very soft. Strain the rice and let it cool. Boil the potato chunks in water, strain, and let them cool.

2. In a bowl, combine the cooked rice, grated carrot, cooked potato, coriander, tomato paste, yeast, and oats. Add salt to taste. Mix until smooth.

3. Shape burgers. Coat with panko. Fry in sunflower oil at 350°F until golden brown.

For the eggplant caviar with cream cheese and herbs:

2 eggplants | 2 cloves garlic, peeled | 2 sprigs of thyme | olive oil | salt | 1 lemon, for zesting | 6 mint leaves, minced | 4 sprigs of chives, minced | 8 ounces Tofutti vegan cream cheese | ½ cup vegan cream

1. Cut the eggplants in half lengthwise and score with a knife. Put the garlic cloves and thyme sprigs in the cuts. Drizzle with olive oil and salt.

Put the halves back together and wrap tightly with foil. Bake at 350°F for 40 minutes.

2. Remove the thyme and garlic from the eggplants. Remove the flesh from the eggplants, chop it up, and add it to a bowl. Zest one-fourth of the lemon. To the eggplant pieces, add lemon zest, mint, chives, vegan cream cheese, and vegan cream. Mix well.

For the toasted hazelnut pesto:

1 cup extra virgin olive oil | 5 toasted hazelnuts | 10 basil leaves | salt

1. Combine all ingredients in a food processor and blend until smooth.

To assemble the burgers:

seeded hamburger buns (appendix)
burgers
eggplant caviar with cream cheese and herbs
toasted hazelnut pesto
2 sprigs of chives, minced
18 basil leaves, sliced

1. Toast the bread in the oven at 350°F. On each bun, place 1 burger, 2 spoonfuls of eggplant caviar, and a drizzle of hazelnut pesto. Garnish with fresh herbs.

Autumn burgers

To make burgers:

water
¼ cup bulgur
½ cauliflower, chopped into florets
olive oil
2 cloves garlic, minced
½ cup small, sweet red peppers
¼ bunch parsley, chopped
½ teaspoon turmeric
¼ cup breadcrumbs
salt and pepper

1. Bring a pot of water to a boil. Add bulgur and cook for 20 minutes. Strain and let cool.

2. Bring another pot of water to a boil. Add the cauliflower florets and cook for 20 minutes. Strain and cool.

3. In a skillet with olive oil, cook the garlic until slightly browned.

4. Pulse the red peppers until finely chopped.

5. In a bowl, combine the chopped peppers, garlic, cauliflower, bulger, parsley, turmeric, breadcrumbs, and salt and pepper to taste. Mix until dough is smooth.

6. Shape burgers. Heat a griddle over medium heat with a little olive oil, and cook the burgers until browned on both sides.

For yellow pepper coulis:

2 yellow peppers | salt

1. Preheat the oven to 350°F. Place peppers on a baking sheet and roast for 40 minutes. Let cool.

2. When peppers are cool enough to handle, peel and seed them. Season with salt to taste. Place in blender or food processor and puree until smooth.

For grilled mushrooms with chili and parsley:

4 large mushroom caps, cleaned and sliced
1 red chile, sliced
2 teaspoons chopped parsley
olive oil | salt

1. In a skillet over high heat, toss mushrooms, chile, parsley, and oil until cooked through. Season with salt to taste.

To assemble the burgers:

bread
sour cream (appendix)
burgers
grilled mushrooms with chili and parsley
yellow pepper coulis

1. Toast the bread in the oven at 350°F.

2. Spread sour cream on the toast. Top with a burger, grilled mushrooms with chili and parsley, and yellow pepper coulis.

Classic veggie burgers

To make classic veggie burgers:

3 onions
3 cups seitan (appendix)
¼ cup breadcrumbs
1 tablespoon nutritional yeast
1 teaspoon mustard
salt and pepper
sunflower oil
vegan mozzarella cheese

1. Preheat oven to 350°F. Wrap onions in foil and bake for 40 minutes. Remove from oven, peel and set aside.

2. In the bowl of a food processor, combine seitan, breadcrumbs, nutritional yeast, mustard, roasted onions, and salt and pepper to taste. Blend until well combined. Transfer to a bowl.

3. Shape the burgers and let stand 5 minutes at room temperature.

4. Heat a griddle over medium heat with a little sunflower oil, and cook the burgers until browned on both sides. Place a slice of cheese on top while cooking to melt.

For the parsley and dill oil:

2 tablespoons fresh dill, chopped
¼ cup fresh parsley
½ clove garlic
½ cup extra virgin olive oil

1. Put all ingredients in a blender and blend until smooth.

To assemble the burgers:

seeded hamburger buns
ketchup (appendix)
classic veggie burger
tomato slices
1 carrot, peeled into ribbons
lettuce
parsley and dill oil

1. Toast buns until golden.

2. Spread a little ketchup on the bottom of each bun. Top with a burger, 2 slices of tomato, carrot ribbons, lettuce, and a drizzle of parsley and dill oil.

OH BOY!

Wild burgers

For burgers:

water
½ cup brown rice
4 spring onions (or sweet onions)
1 cooked beet
handful parsley leaves
2 tablespoons breadcrumbs
salt and pepper
panko | sunflower oil

1. Bring a pot of water to boil. Add the rice and cook 30-40 minutes, following the directions on the package. Strain and set aside to cool.

2. Preheat oven to 400°F.

3. Wrap spring onions in foil and roast for 40 minutes. Turn oven off and let onions sit for 10 more minutes. Peel onions and set aside.

4. In the bowl of a food processor, combine cooked rice, beets, onion, and parsley, and blend until well mixed. Transfer mixture to a bowl. Add 2 tablespoons of breadcrumbs and salt and pepper to taste. Mix well.

5. Shape the burgers. Brush with a little water and dip in panko. Fry in sunflower oil at 375°F for 2 minutes.

For the Romesco mayonnaise:

½ cup Romesco sauce (appendix)
½ cup mayonnaise (appendix)

1. Combine Romesco sauce and mayonnaise in a bowl and mix well.

For sautéed asparagus:

water
1 bunch asparagus, stems removed
olive oil | salt

1. Bring a pot of water to a boil. Add asparagus and cook for 2 minutes. Remove asparagus, and plunge them into a bowl of ice water to stop the cooking.

2. Chop the asparagus and sauté in a skillet over high heat with olive oil. Add salt to taste.

To assemble the burgers:

hamburger buns of stout
scallions, sliced
Romesco mayonnaise
wild burgers
arugula
sautéed asparagus
cherry tomatoes, quartered
extra virgin olive oil
salt and pepper

1. Toast buns on a griddle until well marked.

2. Top each bun with scallions, Romesco mayonnaise, 1 burger, a handful of arugula, sautéed asparagus and cherry tomatoes. Season with olive oil and salt and pepper to taste.

Buckwheat and yellow curry burgers
with sautéed mushrooms

To make buckwheat burgers:

1 cup buckwheat
2 cups vegetable broth
1 onion, diced
1 zucchini, diced
olive oil
8 sprigs of chives, chopped
1 teaspoon yellow curry paste
1 small piece fresh ginger, peeled and grated
2 tablespoons breadcrumbs
salt

1. Combine buckwheat and vegetable broth in a saucepan. Bring to a boil and cook, covered, over low heat for 25 minutes. Strain if there is excess liquid.

2. In a skillet over high heat, sauté onion and zucchini with olive oil for 1 minute.

3. In a large bowl, combine buckwheat, sautéed vegetables, chives, yellow curry paste, ginger and breadcrumbs. Add salt to taste.

4. Shape burgers and cook on griddle with a little olive oil.

For the sautéed mushrooms:

24 black trumpet mushrooms
olive oil
salt

1. In a skillet over high heat, quickly cook the mushrooms with a splash of olive oil, about 30 seconds. Season with salt to taste.

To assemble the burgers:

hamburger buns
apricot ketchup (appendix)
buckwheat burgers
1 zucchini, raw, thinly sliced
spinach
sautéed mushrooms

1. Toast the buns in the oven at 350°F for 30 seconds.

2. Top the toast with a little apricot ketchup, a burger, a few slices of zucchini, spinach, and sautéed mushrooms.

The crown jewel

To make burgers:

1 cup seitan (appendix)
1 clove garlic
1 spring onion
1 teaspoon truffle oil
¼ teaspoon powdered smoke (or liquid smoke or
    smoked paprika)
½ cup TVP | water, or vegetable broth
3 tablespoons breadcrumbs
olive oil | salt and pepper to taste

1. In the bowl of a food processor, combine seitan, garlic, spring onion, truffle oil, and powdered smoke. Blend until well mixed. Transfer mixture to a bowl.

2. Soak TVP in water or vegetable broth until well hydrated. Strain to remove excess liquid.

3. Add hydrated TVP to the seitan mixture along with breadcrumbs, 2 tablespoons of olive oil, and salt and pepper to taste. Mix well.

4. Shape the burgers. Heat a griddle over medium heat with a little olive oil, and cook the burgers until browned on both sides.

For grilled mushrooms:

¼ bunch parsley
1 clove garlic
olive oil | ½ cayenne pepper
salt | 8 mushrooms, sliced

1. In a blender, puree the parsley, garlic, ½ cup olive oil, cayenne, and salt until smooth.

2. In a skillet over medium heat, cook the mushrooms until browned. Season with the oil from the blender.

For avocado with lime:

1 avocado | juice of 1 lime | salt

1. Slice open the avocado and scoop out the flesh. In a bowl, combine the avocado and lime juice. Mash until smooth, and season with salt to taste.

To assemble the burgers:

sun-dried tomato roll (appendix)
mayonnaise (appendix)
avocado with lime
seitan burgers
grilled mushrooms
patatas bravas (appendix)

1. Toast rolls in the oven at 350°F for 30 seconds.

2. On each roll, spread a little mayonnaise, avocado, a burger, and top with mushrooms. Serve with *patatas bravas*.

Sweet potato burgers
with Thai salad

To make sweet potato and peanut patties:

1¼ tablespoons TVP
water, or vegetable broth
2 sweet potatoes
1¼ tablespoons cooked corn
¼ bunch cilantro, chopped
1¼ tablespoons salted peanuts, chopped
¼ teaspoon chili | salt | sunflower oil

1. Soak TVP in water or vegetable broth until well hydrated. Strain to remove excess liquid.

2. Preheat oven to 350°F. Bake sweet potatoes until very tender. Remove skins and place potatoes in a bowl.

3. Add corn, chopped cilantro, peanuts, chili, and hydrated TVP to the potatoes. Mix well. Add salt to taste.

4. Shape the burgers. Heat a griddle over medium heat with a little sunflower oil, and cook the burgers until browned on both sides.

For the Thai salad:

¼ cabbage, or bok choy, thinly sliced
2 carrots, grated
juice of 1 lime
4 tablespoons sour Thai sauce (appendix)
4 sprigs of chives, chopped
¼ teaspoon salt

1. Combine ingredients in a bowl and mix well.

For wasabi mayonnaise:

½ cup mayonnaise (appendix)
½ teaspoon wasabi powder

1. Mix the mayonnaise with the wasabi powder. Store in refrigerator.

To assemble the burgers:

soft burger buns (appendix)
wasabi mayonnaise
sweet potato burgers
tomato, sliced
Thai salad
onion rings (appendix)

1. Toast the buns. Cut in half.

2. On bottom bun, spread some wasabi mayonnaise. Top with a burger, two slices of tomato, and some Thai salad. Serve with onion rings.

Southern burgers
with fennel

To make burgers:

5 potatoes
1 head of garlic
2 tomatoes, chopped
olive oil
salt and pepper

1. Bake the potatoes in the oven at 350°F until tender. Peel them and set aside.

2. Bake head of garlic at 350°F for 20 minutes.

3. Sauté tomatoes in a pan with a little olive oil over medium heat until they release some water.

4. Peel the garlic cloves and add to a blender with the tomatoes.

5. Add the potatoes to the garlic and tomatoes. Puree thoroughly until smooth. Add salt and pepper to taste.

6. Shape burgers. Heat a griddle over medium heat with a little olive oil and cook the burgers until browned on both sides.

For the marinated fennel:

juice of 2 lemons
4 leaves of mint
salt
1 fennel bulb, thinly sliced

1. Combine lemon juice, mint, and salt in small bowl, and let stand overnight.

2. Add the fennel and marinate for two hours.

To assemble the burgers:

tomato
olive oil
salt
soft burger buns (appendix)
mayonnaise (appendix)
burgers
marinated fennel
baked potato
mojo (appendix)

1. Cut the tomatoes into small cubes and leave them in olive oil and salt.

2. Toast the bottom of the bread on a griddle with a little olive oil.

3. Spread a spoonful of mayonnaise on the toast. Top with a burger, some marinated fennel, and the diced tomato. Serve with a baked potato and a little mojo.

APPENDIX
Condiments, Sauces, Breads, and Sides

Seitan

To make the dough:

¼ cup flour
4½ cups wheat gluten
5½ cups water

1. Mix flour with gluten in a bowl. Add water and knead until dough is smooth with no lumps.

2. Let stand for 30 minutes covered with plastic wrap or cloth to keep it moist. This step is very important because it will make sure the gluten is well hydrated and won't fall apart when simmered. Once it is rested, shape it into several balls about 2 inches in diameter.

3. Fill a large pot three-fourths-full with water and bring to a boil. Add the seitan balls and reduce heat to medium. Simmer for an hour.

To make the broth:

water | 2 cups soy sauce | 1 ginger root | 2 heads of garlic | 1 carrot | 1 leek | 1 celery | 1 onion | 4 sprigs rosemary | 1 sprig thyme | 1 teaspoon smoked salt | 2 tablespoons brown sugar | 1 cup red wine

1. Fill a large pot halfway with water. Add the remaining ingredients and bring it to a boil.

2. Simmer seitan balls in the broth for 50 minutes. Store the seitan in a container with broth for 24 hours in the refrigerator.

3. Seitan keeps in the fridge for 4–5 days. If you will not be using it within that time frame, freeze the container.

Ketchup

1¾ cups crushed tomatoes
1⅓ cups brown sugar
½ cup white wine vinegar
⅓ cup water | ⅓ cup agave syrup
1 teaspoon paprika
2 cloves garlic, chopped
1 leek, chopped
¼ celery | ½ teaspoon salt

1. Combine all ingredients in a pot and bring to a boil. Cook over low heat for 30 minutes, stirring every few minutes.

2. Store ketchup in sterilized jars or a container.

Apricot ketchup

2 apricots | 1⅓ cups crushed tomatoes | 1 cup apple cider vinegar | 1 cup brown sugar | 1 teaspoon grated fresh ginger | ¼ teaspoon nutmeg | ¼ cayenne pepper | ½ teaspoon salt

1. Peel and pit the apricots, then cut into small pieces.

2. Combine all ingredients in a pot and bring to a boil. Cover and cook on low for 20 minutes, stirring every few minutes.

3. If the sauce is still runny, cook another 10 minutes uncovered until liquid evaporates. Otherwise, blend it and store immediately in sterilized jars or in a container.

Ketchup

BBQ sauce

1⅓ cups crushed tomatoes
1 teaspoon grated fresh ginger
2 red onions
1⅓ cups brown sugar
1⅓ cups balsamic vinegar
½ teaspoon salt
1 teaspoon smoked salt
4 leaves of basil, sliced

1. Combine all ingredients (except basil) in a pot and bring to a boil. Cover and cook over low heat for 20 minutes, stirring every few minutes.

2. Stir in the basil and store in sterilized jars or container in fridge.

Chipotle BBQ sauce

1⅓ cups crushed tomatoes
2 red onions, diced
1⅓ cups brown sugar
1⅓ cups balsamic vinegar
½ teaspoon salt
1 teaspoon smoked salt
¼ cup cilantro
1 chipotle pepper in adobo, chopped

1. Combine all ingredients (except cilantro and chipotle pepper) together in a pot, and bring to a boil.

2. Cover and cook over low heat for 20 minutes, stirring every few minutes.

3. After 20 minutes, stir in cilantro and chipotle. Store in sterilized jars or container in refrigerator.

Strawberry BBQ sauce

2 cups strawberries, washed, trimmed, and sliced
1 cup brown sugar
1 leek
1 red onion
2 cups balsamic vinegar
½ teaspoon salt
1 teaspoon smoked salt
6 sprigs rosemary

1. Combine all ingredients in a pot and bring to a boil.

2. Cover pot and cook over low heat for 20 minutes, stirring every few minutes.

3. After 20 minutes, store in sterilized jars or container in fridge.

Saté sauce

2 cloves garlic, chopped
1 onion, diced
2 teaspoons grated fresh ginger
2 tablespoons sunflower oil
1 tablespoon brown sugar
½ cayenne pepper
1½ cups water
2 tablespoons peanut butter
1 lime, for zesting
¾ teaspoon salt

1. In a pan over medium heat, cook the garlic, onion, and ginger with sunflower oil until golden.

2. Add the sugar, cayenne, water, peanut butter, a pinch of the lime zest, and salt. Bring to a boil and cook over low heat for 10 minutes.

3. Transfer to a blender or use an immersion blender, and blend until you have a smooth consistency. Store in sterilized jars or container.

Romesco sauce

1 head of garlic
6 ripe tomatoes, halved
1¼ tablespoons toasted hazelnuts
2 tablespoons toasted almonds
2 tablespoons roasted nuts
1 hydrated cherry pepper
½ cup apple cider vinegar
½ cup olive oil
1 tablespoon paprika
1 teaspoon salt

1. Preheat oven to 350°F. Place garlic and tomatoes on a tray and roast for 20 minutes.

2. Peel tomatoes and garlic and put them in the bowl of a food processor. Add remaining ingredients and blend until smooth. Store in sterilized jars or container.

Roasted red pepper sauce

1 red pepper
½ cup crushed tomatoes
¼ cup olive oil
½ cup vegetable broth
1 teaspoon spicy smoked paprika
1 tablespoon paprika
1 teaspoon salt

1. Preheat oven to 350°F. Put red pepper on a pan and roast for 30 minutes. Peel and seed the pepper.

2. In a pot, combine the peeled pepper with the remaining ingredients and cook for 15 minutes over low heat until the broth is reduced by half. Store in sterilized jars or container.

Mayonnaise

⅓ cup soy milk (without sugar and flavorings)
½ cup sunflower oil
½ teaspoon salt
juice of 1 lemon

1. Combine soy milk, sunflower oil, and salt in a blender and blend until smooth.

2. Add lemon juice and blend.

Chipotle mayonnaise

⅓ cup soy milk (without sugar or flavorings)
½ cup sunflower oil
1 lemon
½ clove garlic
½ chipotle chile
½ teaspoon paprika
½ teaspoon salt

1. Combine ingredients in a blender and blend until smooth.

Light mayonnaise

1 cup natural tofu
1 tablespoon apple cider vinegar
2 tablespoons sunflower oil
½ clove garlic
½ teaspoon salt

1. Combine all ingredients in a blender and blend until smooth.

Japanese mayonnaise

½ cup soy milk
¾ cup sunflower oil
1 teaspoon Dijon mustard
1 tablespoon sugar
1 lime
1 teaspoon white miso
1 teaspoon vinegar

1. Combine ingredients in a blender and blend until smooth.

Macadamia and tofu mayonnaise

½ cup raw macadamia nuts
water
½ cup soft tofu
1 tablespoon apple cider vinegar
3 tablespoons sunflower oil
½ clove garlic
½ teaspoon salt

1. Soak macadamia nuts over night, changing water every 8 hours.

2. Drain macadamia nuts. Combine all ingredients in a blender and blend until smooth.

Aioli

water
1 cup garlic cloves, peeled
2 cups olive oil
juice of 1 lemon
1 teaspoon salt

1. Bring a saucepan of water to boil. Add the garlic and cook for 1 minute. Strain and put garlic in cold water. Blend garlic until smooth.

2. Add oil slowly in a thin stream while blending, add the lemon juice and salt. Store in refrigerator.

Chipotle mayonnaise

Tartar sauce

To make mayonnaise:

⅓ cup soy milk (without sugar and flavorings)
½ cup sunflower oil
½ teaspoon salt
juice of 1 lemon

1. Combine soy milk, oil, and salt in a blender and blend until smooth.

2. Add lemon juice and blend.

To make the tartar sauce:

1 teaspoon Dijon mustard
6 capers, chopped
3 pickles, chopped
mayonnaise

1. Mix mustard, capers, and pickles into the mayonnaise. Stir well to combine.

Vegan deluxe sauce

To make mayonnaise:

⅓ cup soy milk (without sugar and flavorings)
½ cup sunflower oil
½ teaspoon salt
juice of 1 lemon

1. Combine soy milk, sunflower oil, and salt in a blender and blend until smooth.

2. Add lemon juice and blend well.

To make the vegan deluxe sauce:

¼ cup Tofutti vegan cream cheese
Vegan mayonnaise
3 tablespoons vegan cream
1 clove garlic, chopped
juice of 1 lemon
1 teaspoon apple cider vinegar
¼ teaspoon salt
¼ teaspoon pepper

1. With an electric mixer, beat the cream cheese and vegan mayonnaise together until smooth.

2. Add the vegan cream, garlic, lemon juice, vinegar, salt, and pepper. Whisk until smooth.

Thai sweet and sour sauce

2 Thai chili peppers, chopped
4 cloves garlic, chopped
1 teaspoon grated fresh ginger
½ cup sugar
¾ cup water
¼ cup coconut milk
½ cup apple cider vinegar
½ cup crushed tomatoes (optional)
1 tablespoon cornstarch, diluted with 2 tablespoons water

1. Combine all ingredients except for cornstarch in a saucepan. Cook over low heat for 15 minutes. Stir in cornstarch slurry and stir until thick. Remove from heat and store in fridge.

Vegan Worcestershire sauce

1 cup apple cider vinegar
⅓ cup soy sauce
½ cup brown sugar
1 teaspoon Dijon mustard
1 clove garlic
½ teaspoon grated fresh ginger
2 leaves of basil, sliced

1. Combine all ingredients except basil in a saucepan and bring to a boil. Cook, covered, for 20 minutes over low heat. Remove from heat and stir in basil.

Dill mustard

2 tablespoons Dijon mustard
2 tablespoons apple cider vinegar
⅓ cup sunflower oil
1¼ tablespoons agave syrup
1 teaspoon salt
4 sprigs dill, chopped

1. Combine all ingredients except dill in the bowl of a food processor. Blend until smooth. Stir in dill.

Vegan sour cream

1⅓ cups soft tofu
2 tablespoons sunflower oil
juice of 2 lemons
1 tablespoon apple cider vinegar
1 tablespoon agave syrup
1 teaspoon salt

1. Combine all ingredients in the bowl of a food processor. Blend until smooth. Store in refrigerator.

Tzatziki sauce

⅓ cup olive oil
¾ cup natural soy yogurt
½ cup Tofutti vegan cream cheese
juice of 1 lemon
2 cloves garlic, chopped
1 teaspoon dill, chopped
1 cucumber, grated
1 teaspoon salt

1. Whisk together olive oil, yogurt and cream cheese. Add lemon juice, garlic, and dill. Whisk until well blended.

2. Add the grated cucumber and salt, and stir well. Let stand for a few hours in the refrigerator.

Vegan cheese sauce

4 cups raw cashews
water
½ cup lemon juice
4 tablespoons nutritional yeast
2 teaspoons salt

1. Soak cashews in 1 cup of water overnight, or for at least 8 hours. Strain.

2. Combine all ingredients in the bowl of a food processor and blend until smooth. Add ½ cup of water to make a looser sauce.

Mojo

½ cup olive oil
1 head of garlic, chopped
1 tablespoon paprika
½ teaspoon cumin
1 tablespoon apple cider vinegar
1 cayenne pepper
2 tablespoons breadcrumbs
1 teaspoon salt

1. In a pan over medium heat, cook the garlic in the olive oil until golden. Add the remaining ingredients and cook for 2 minutes. Transfer mixture to food processor.

2. Pulse until a chunky sauce forms.

Pico de gallo

8 tomatoes, diced, seeds removed
2 red onions or scallions, diced
1 teaspoon chopped cilantro
juice of 1 lime
1 teaspoon salt

1. Mix ingredients in a bowl with lime juice and salt to taste. Store in refrigerator until ready to use.

Eggplant caviar

2 eggplants
2 cloves garlic, peeled
2 sprigs fresh thyme
¼ cup olive oil
1 package of Tofutti vegan cream cheese
2 teaspoons salt
½ teaspoon pepper
water

1. Cut the eggplants in half lengthwise and score with a knife. Put the garlic cloves and thyme sprigs in the cuts. Drizzle with olive oil and salt. Put the halves back together and wrap tightly with foil. Bake at 350°F for 40 minutes.

2. Remove the thyme and garlic from the eggplants. Scoop the flesh from the eggplants, and place in a bowl with the vegan cream cheese, salt, pepper, and a little water. Mix well.

Eggplant caviar

Chimichurri

½ cup sunflower oil
¼ cup red wine vinegar
¼ cup chopped garlic
2 cups chopped parsley
½ cup chopped cilantro
2 tablespoons chopped oregano
¼ cup red pepper
¼ teaspoon pepper
1 teaspoon salt

1. Combine all ingredients and mix well.

Teriyaki sauce

½ cup soy sauce
½ cup water
¼ cup rice vinegar
⅓ cup brown sugar
1 teaspoon grated fresh ginger
2 cloves garlic, chopped
1 tablespoon cornstarch diluted in 2 tablespoons
    water

1. In a saucepan over medium heat, combine all ingredients except cornstarch. Bring to a boil, stirring.

2. Once at a boil, stir in cornstarch. Cook over medium heat until thick. Remove from heat and store in refrigerator.

Tahini sauce

¾ cup roasted sesame seeds
3 tablespoons sunflower oil
½ cup water
2 cloves garlic, chopped
juice of 1 lemon
1 teaspoon salt
mint leaves, chopped, for garnish (optional)
additional toasted sesame seeds, for garnish
    (optional)

1. Mix ingredients together until smooth. Garnish with mint and more sesame seeds if desired.

Hummus

2¼ cups cooked chickpeas
2 cloves garlic
½ teaspoon ground cumin
2 tablespoons tahini
juice of 2 lemons
2 tablespoons olive oil
½ cup water
1 teaspoon salt
½ teaspoon pepper

1. In a blender or food processor, blend the chickpeas, garlic, cumin, tahini, lemon juice, oil, water, salt, and pepper until you have a smooth paste. Serve at room temperature.

Tahini sauce

Baba ganoush

3 eggplants
1 cup natural soy yogurt
juice of 1 lemon
3 cloves garlic
3 tablespoons roasted tahini
3 tablespoons olive oil
1 teaspoon salt

1. Prick eggplants with a fork and cook directly over the fire (no pan or iron), so the skin is charred and the center is very tender. Let eggplant cool on a plate.

2. Blend soy yogurt, lemon juice, garlic, tahini, olive oil, and salt until creamy smooth.

3. Remove the eggplant pulp from the skins (discard skins), and blend with the cream. Serve at room temperature.

Roasted garlic

3 heads garlic

1. Wrap the garlic cloves in foil and place on a baking sheet. Bake at 350°F for 30 minutes. Let cool to room temperature.

2. Remove the foil, peel the garlic cloves, and use them whole, chopped, or pureed.

Pickles

1 cup small cucumbers
2⅓ cups water
2⅓ cups apple cider vinegar
1 teaspoon salt
1 tablespoon brown sugar
1 piece of fresh ginger

1. Combine ingredients in a pot and bring to a boil. Cook for 5 minutes over low heat.

2. Store cucumbers in liquid in the fridge for 3 days before serving.

Herb-infused olive oil

1 cup extra virgin olive oil
1 sprig rosemary (or other herb)

1. Combine olive oil and herbs in a saucepan over low heat. Warm until oil reaches 120°F. Maintain this temperature for 25 minutes.

2. Store oil and herbs in a sterilized glass jar for 3 weeks at room temperature.

Vegetable broth

1 stalk celery, chopped
1 bay leaf
2 onions, chopped
1 leek, cleaned and chopped
2 carrots, chopped
2 parsnips, chopped
1 head of garlic, cloves peeled and chopped
4 leaves of parsley
3 sprigs thyme
water

1. In a large pot, combine all ingredients and cover with water. Bring to a boil. Cover and lower heat, cooking for 3 hours.

2. Strain broth and season with salt.

Mushroom broth

4 onions, chopped
1 leek, cleaned and chopped
3 tablespoons olive oil
10 shiitake mushrooms, chopped
2 porcini mushrooms, chopped
2 sage leaves | water | salt

1. In a large pot over medium heat, brown the onion and leek in a little olive oil. Add the mushrooms and sage, and cook for an additional 10 minutes over low heat.

2. Add water to cover and bring to a boil. Simmer for 3 hours over low heat. Strain broth and season with a pinch of salt.

Soft burger bun (large or small)

1¼ cups warm water | 2 tablespoons yeast | 2¼ cups bread flour | 1 tablespoon salt | 2 tablespoons sugar | ¼ cup extra virgin olive oil | sesame seeds

1. In a small bowl, add the warm water and sprinkle with yeast. In a large bowl, mix together the flour, salt, and sugar. Stir in the water and yeast. Knead together for 5 minutes. Add the oil and knead for 15 minutes more until dough is smooth and elastic.

2. Cover bowl with plastic wrap and leave at room temperature until doubled in size.

3. After dough has doubled, punch it down and divide into 2-ounce pieces (for large buns) or 1-ounce pieces (for small buns). Place pieces on a tray, cover with a damp cloth, and let rise until doubled in size.

4. Brush the rolls with water and sprinkle with sesame seeds. Bake at 400°F until golden.

Sun-dried tomato rolls (large or small)

1¼ cups water | 2 tablespoons yeast | 2¼ cups bread flour | 1 tablespoon salt | 2 tablespoons sugar | ¼ cup extra virgin olive oil | 1¼ tablespoons sun-dried tomatoes, chopped

1. In a small bowl, add the water and sprinkle with yeast.

2. In a large bowl, mix together the flour, salt, sugar, and slowly add the water with yeast. Knead for 5 minutes. Add the oil and knead for 15 minutes. Cover the bowl with plastic wrap and let rise at room temperature until doubled in size.

3. Knead in the sun-dried tomatoes. Divide dough into 2-ounce pieces (large rolls) or 1-ounce pieces (small rolls). Place pieces on a tray, cover with a damp cloth, and let rise until doubled in size.

4. Brush rolls with water. Bake at 400°F until golden brown.

Onion rolls with nuts and dried apricots (large or small)

1¼ cups water | 2 tablespoons yeast | 2¼ cups bread flour | 1 tablespoon salt | 2 tablespoons sugar | ¼ cup extra virgin olive oil | 1 spring onion, sliced | 2 tablespoons walnuts, chopped | 1¼ tablespoons chopped dried apricots

1. In a small bowl, add the water and sprinkle with yeast.

2. In a large bowl, mix the flour, salt, sugar, and slowly add the water with yeast. Knead for 5 minutes. Add the oil and continue kneading for 15 minutes. Cover the bowl with plastic wrap and let rise at room temperature until doubled in size.

3. Knead in the onion, walnuts, and apricots. Divide dough into 2-ounce pieces (for large rolls) or 1-ounce pieces (for small rolls). Place rolls on a tray, cover with a damp cloth, and let rise until doubled in size.

4. Brush the rolls with water and bake at 400°F until golden brown.

Rosemary rolls (large or small)

3 sprigs rosemary | ⅓ cup extra virgin olive oil | 1¼ cups water | 2 tablespoons yeast | 2¼ cups bread flour | 2 tablespoons salt | 2 tablespoons sugar

1. Remove leaves from sprigs of rosemary. Crush rosemary in oil until a paste forms.

2. In a small bowl, add the water and sprinkle with yeast.

3. In a large bowl, mix the flour, salt, sugar, and slowly add the water with yeast. Knead for 5 minutes. Add the rosemary oil and knead for 15 minutes. Cover the bowl with plastic wrap and let rise at room temperature until doubled in size.

4. Punch down dough. Divide into 2-ounce pieces (for large rolls), or 1-ounce pieces (for small rolls). Place rolls on tray, cover with damp cloth, and let rise until doubled in size.

5. Brush rolls with water. Bake at 400°F until golden brown.

Pizza dough

1 cup water | 1 tablespoon yeast | 1¾ cups bread flour | ¾ tablespoon sugar | 1 tablespoon salt | 2 tablespoons extra virgin olive oil | 1 teaspoon cornmeal

1. In a small bowl add the water and sprinkle with yeast.

2. In a large bowl, mix the flour, sugar, salt, oil, and water with yeast. Knead for 10 minutes until dough is smooth and sticky.

3. Cover bowl with plastic wrap and let rise until doubled in size.

4. Sprinkle cornmeal on countertop to prevent sticking. Shape dough into a ball, or several smaller balls, and stretch into desired shape.

Onion rings

To make the batter:

2 tablespoons cornstarch | ⅓ cup water | 2⅓ cups wheat flour | 1 teaspoon baking powder | 1 teaspoon salt | ½ teaspoon pepper | 1⅓ cups beer

1. Stir cornstarch and water together to make a slurry.

2. In a large bowl, mix together flour, baking powder, salt, and pepper. Stir in the beer and the cornstarch slurry. Whisk well.

For the onion rings:

sunflower oil | 1 onion, sliced into rings | batter | panko

1. In a large pot, heat oil to 350°F.

2. Dip onions first into batter and then into panko so they are thoroughly coated. Fry in oil until they are golden brown on both sides.

Baked sweet potato strips

1 sweet potato | 1 teaspoon salt | ¼ teaspoon pepper | 3 tablespoons extra virgin olive oil

1. Peel the sweet potatoes and cut into strips.

2. In a large bowl, toss potatoes with salt, pepper, and olive oil.

3. Put potatoes in a baking dish and cover with foil. Bake at 350°F for 20 minutes.

4. Remove the foil and bake for 15 more minutes until brown.

Thick-cut fries

2 potatoes, cut into large fries | salt | olive oil

1. Toss potatoes with salt and let stand for 30 minutes.

2. In a large pot, heat oil to 350°F.

3. Fry potatoes until lightly browned. Let cool and re-fry until golden brown.

Patatas bravas

Grilled potatoes

2 potatoes, thinly sliced
olive oil
salt

1. On a griddle over low heat with a little olive oil, place potato slices in a single layer. Make sure the potatoes' surfaces are all touching the pan. Cook, covered, over low heat until potatoes begin to brown.

2. Flip potatoes and cook the other side until golden. Season with salt.

Baked potatoes

2 large potatoes
salt
pepper

1. Preheat oven to 350°F.

2. Put potatoes in a pot of water with a pinch of salt. Bring to a boil and simmer for 10 minutes.

3. Place potatoes on a baking sheet and bake for 20 minutes. Cut open and serve with salt and pepper to taste, or with additional toppings such as sour cream or butter.

Patatas bravas

sunflower oil
2 potatoes, peeled and diced
salt
hot sauce

1. In a large pot, heat oil to 200°F.

2. Fry potatoes for 15 minutes. Drain and cool. Season with salt.

3. Bring temperature of oil up to 350°F. Fry potatoes again until browned.

4. Serve with hot sauce, or aioli with smoked paprika and nutmeg.

Fries

3 potatoes, peeled and cut into sticks.
salt
sunflower oil

1. In a large pot, add potatoes and cover with water. Bring to a boil and simmer for 5 minutes.

2. Strain potatoes and dry well. Add salt and let cool.

3. Heat oil to 350°F. Fry potatoes until they are golden.

4. Serve with ketchup or your favorite sauce.

Purple potatoes with Romesco sauce

sunflower oil | 4 purple potatoes, cut into half moons | salt | Romesco sauce (see appendix) |

1. In a frying pan, heat oil to 350°F. Pre-heat oven to 325°F.

2. Fry potatoes until they begin to brown, but are not soft.

3. Spread potatoes on a baking sheet. Sprinkle with salt and bake for 15 minutes

4. Serve with Romesco sauce and chopped chives.

Roasted artichokes

4 artichokes | ¾ cup olive oil | ¾ cup sunflower oil | 1 head of garlic | salt

1. Heat oven to 350°F.

2. Remove the tough outer leaves of the artichokes and remove stems. Cut in half from top to bottom.

3. Pour olive and sunflower oils into a baking dish. Put the artichokes cut-side down in the dish. Add the garlic cloves. Cover with foil and bake for 20 minutes.

4. Remove foil and bake another 10 minutes until very tender.

Delicious Desserts

Rice pudding "burgers"
with strawberries

For creamy rice pudding:

1 quart soy milk
¾ cup sugar
1 cinnamon stick
rind of ½ lemon
1⅓ cups white rice
8 ounces Tofutti vegan cream cheese

1. Combine soy milk, sugar, cinnamon stick, and lemon rind in a saucepan. Bring to a boil over medium heat, then lower heat and simmer.

2. Rinse rice in cold water until water runs clear to remove excess starch.

3. Add the rice to the simmering soy milk and cook on low for 40 minutes. Once the rice is cooked, remove the lemon rind and cinnamon stick.

4. Stir in the cream cheese and stir vigorously until melted.

5. Place ring molds on a platter and portion out the rice pudding. Let cool in the refrigerator.

To assemble burgers:

8 pieces of chocolate-and-candied-orange bread
creamy rice pudding
2 cups rice milk
pint of strawberries, quartered

1. Top each slice of bread with a rice pudding patty, a little rice milk, and the strawberries.

Coca de forner
with frozen yogurt and toffee

For frozen yogurt:

3½ cups unsweetened soy yogurt
⅓ cup agave syrup

1. Mix together soy yogurt and agave syrup. Pour into ice cream maker and churn for 15–20 minutes.

2. If you do not have an ice cream maker, mix yogurt and syrup in a container, place in freezer and whisk every 10 minutes. Do this 8 times.

To make the toffee sauce:

1 cup sugar
1 cup water
1⅓ cups vegan cream
⅓ cup orange juice

1. Combine sugar and water in saucepan and cook until caramelized.

2. Add cream and orange juice, and cook for a few seconds until well combined.

To assemble:

coca de forner **(made with olive oil, not lard)**
frozen yogurt
toffee sauce

1. Slice the *forner* into 16 pieces.

2. Plate 8 slices and top with a scoop of frozen yogurt and a drizzle of toffee sauce. Top with another slice of *forner*.

Gingersnaps
with praline ice cream

For ice cream:

2 cups rice milk | 1 cinnamon stick | ⅓ cup sugar | ¾ cup almond pralines

---

1. In a saucepan over medium heat, combine rice milk, cinnamon stick, and sugar and bring to a boil.

2. Strain the mixture and transfer to blender with pralines. Blend until well combined and store in refrigerator for 3 hours.

3. Pour the cooled rice milk mixture into an ice cream maker and let churn for 15–20 minutes. Or, if you don't have an ice cream maker, pour rice milk into container and keep in freezer, whisking every 10 minutes. Do this 8 times.

To make the gingersnaps:

1⅓ cups margarine, melted | ¼ cup almond meal | 1⅓ cups castor sugar | 5¼ cups flour | 1 tablespoon salt | ¼ teaspoon ground cloves | ¼ teaspoon ground ginger | ½ cup candied almonds

---

1. In a large bowl, combine all ingredients except the almonds.

2. Mix well until smooth dough is formed. Cover with plastic wrap and refrigerate until cold.

3. Roll dough to ¼-inch thickness. Sprinkle with almonds, and return to refrigerator for 30 minutes.

4. Cut cookies with a cookie cutter and bake at 350°F until golden brown.

To assemble:

**gingersnaps
ice cream**

---

1. Plate each cookie and top with a scoop of ice cream. Top with another cookie and press. Scrape edges with a spatula to even out the ice cream.

Pistachio cookies
with chocolate cream and raspberry jam

To make pistachio cookie:

½ tablespoon salt
3¼ cups sugar
2 cups flour
1 cup margarine
¼ cup cornstarch
⅓ cup water
1 tablespoon vanilla extract
½ cup shelled and chopped pistachios

1. In a large bowl, combine the salt, sugar, and flour. Add margarine and mix well until the mixture resembles crumbs.

2. In a small bowl, mix together the cornstarch and water to form a slurry. Stir cornstarch slurry into the crumbly dough. Mix well, adding vanilla.

3. Form dough into 16 balls, and place them on a baking sheet. Flatten each ball, adding a pinch of crushed pistachios. Roll the edges over the pistachios to seal.

4. Bake cookies at 350°F until edges are crisp, about 12 minutes.

For the chocolate cream:

1⅓ cups vegan cream
1⅓ cups dark chocolate

1. In a saucepan over medium heat, bring the vegan cream to a boil. Add the chocolate and whisk until melted.

2. Keep cream in a container covered with plastic wrap in the refrigerator.

To assemble:

pistachio cookies
chocolate cream
raspberry jam
freeze-dried raspberries

1. Plate half of the cookies. Top each with a quenelle of chocolate cream and a dollop of raspberry jam. Sprinkle with freeze-dried raspberries and top with another cookie.

Dark chocolate cookies
with hazelnut ice cream

To make cookies:

½ tablespoon salt
3¼ cups sugar
2 cups flour
1 cup margarine
¼ cup cornstarch
⅓ cup water
1 tablespoon vanilla extract
¾ cup chopped dark chocolate

1. In a large bowl, combine salt, sugar, and flour. Add margarine and mix well until dough resembles crumbs.

2. In a small bowl, dilute the cornstarch with the water and add to the flour mixture. Mix well, adding vanilla extract. Stir in the chopped chocolate.

3. Shape dough into 16 balls and place on a baking sheet. Press to flatten slightly.

4. Bake cookies at 350°F until edges are crisp, about 12 minutes.

For hazelnut ice cream:

2 cups rice milk
1 vanilla bean, scraped
⅓ cup sugar
¾ cup crushed hazelnut pralines

1. In a saucepan over medium heat, combine rice, vanilla, and sugar. Bring to a boil. Strain and add to a blender with the hazelnut pralines. Blend until smooth and transfer to refrigerator for 3 hours.

2. Pour the cooled rice milk into an ice cream maker and churn for 15–20 minutes. Or if you do not have an ice cream maker, put milk in a container in the freezer, whisking every 10 minutes. Do this 8 times.

To assemble:

dark chocolate cookie
hazelnut ice cream
chopped toasted hazelnuts

1. Plate half of the cookies. Top each with hazelnut ice cream, and then another cookie. Press together and scrape edges to smooth. Roll edges of sandwiches in chopped hazelnuts.

Caramel waffle cookies
with strawberry ice cream

For the strawberry ice cream:

2⅓ cups strawberries
1¾ cups unsweetened soy yogurt
⅓ cup agave syrup

1. Place strawberries in blender and puree. Drain to extract seeds, reserving liquid.

2. In a bowl, combine the strawberry puree with yogurt and agave. Pour into an ice cream maker and churn for 15–20 minutes. Or if you don't have an ice cream maker, pour yogurt into container and place in freezer, whisking every 10 minutes. Do this 8 times.

For the berry coulis:

1 cup frozen berries
1¼ tablespoons brown sugar
juice of 1 lemon

1. Combine frozen berries and brown sugar in a bowl, cover it, and refrigerate overnight.

2. The next day, transfer berries to a saucepan and bring to a boil over medium heat. Remove from heat and stir in lemon juice. Return to refrigerator.

To assemble:

16 caramel waffle cookies
strawberry ice cream
berry coulis

1. Plate half the waffle cookies. Top each with a scoop of ice cream, a spoonful of berry coulis, and top with another cookie.

Apple and banana smoothies
with vanilla ice cream and cinnamon

For apple smoothie:

6 apples
⅓ cup brown sugar
juice 1 lemon
¾ cup rice milk
ice cubes

1. Peel and core the apples. Slice into half moons. On a baking sheet lined with parchment, spread the apple slices and sprinkle brown sugar on top. Bake at 350°F for 20 minutes. Transfer to refrigerator to cool for 2 hours.

2. Combine apples, lemon juice, rice milk, and a few ice cubes in a blender. Blend until smooth. Pour into 8 glasses.

For banana smoothie:

3 bananas, peeled
1¼ tablespoons agave syrup
1⅓ cups rice milk
ice cubes

1. Combine bananas, agave, rice milk, and a few ice cubes in a blender. Blend until smooth.

For vanilla ice cream:

3½ cups vegan cream
¾ cup sugar
2 vanilla beans, split and scraped

1. In a saucepan, combine vegan cream, sugar, and vanilla. Over medium heat, bring to a boil. Remove from heat and cover with plastic wrap. Let stand for 1 hour to let the vanilla infuse the milk thoroughly. Transfer to refrigerator.

2. Once cooled, strain to remove vanilla. Pour mixture into ice cream maker and churn for 15–20 minutes. Or if you do not have an ice cream maker, place mixture in refrigerator in a container, whisking every 10 minutes; do this 8 times.

To assemble:

apple smoothie
banana smoothie
vanilla ice cream
cinnamon

1. Into the same glass with the apple smoothies, carefully spoon the banana smoothie on top. Add a scoop of vanilla ice cream and sprinkle with cinnamon.

Apricot smoothies
with chocolate, chestnuts, and rum

For apricot smoothie:

10 apricots, pitted
1⅓ cups rice milk
ice cubes

1. Combine apricots and rice milk in a blender with a few ice cubes and blend until smooth. Pour into 8 cups.

For the chocolate sauce:

1⅓ cups rice milk
⅓ cup agave syrup
⅓ cup dark chocolate
ice cubes

1. In a saucepan over medium heat, combine rice milk and agave, and bring to a boil. Stir in chocolate until melted. Transfer to blender and blend until smooth. Add a few ice cubes and blend again.

For rum-chestnut smoothie:

2 cups soy milk
¼ cup sweetened chestnut puree
3 tablespoons rum
ice cubes

1. Combine soy milk, chestnut puree, and rum in a blender. Blend until smooth.

2. Add a few ice cubes and puree again.

To assemble:

apricot smoothie
chocolate sauce
chestnuts and rum puree

1. Carefully top each cup of apricot smoothie with chocolate sauce.

2. Spoon some of the chestnut and rum puree on top.

Cookies and cream milkshakes
with strawberry foam

For chocolate milkshake:

⅓ cup dark chocolate
2½ cups soy milk at room temperature
¼ cup agave syrup
ice cubes

1. In a double boiler, melt chocolate until it is about 120°F.

2. Combine the soy milk, agave, and melted chocolate in a blender and blend until smooth. Add a few ice cubes and puree again.

3. Pour the mixture into 8 glasses.

For cookies-and-cream milkshake:

16 Oreo cookies
1¾ cups vegan cream

1. Combine the cookies and cream in a blender and pulse until chopped.

2. Carefully pour the cookie mixture on top of the chocolate milkshake.

For strawberry foam:

1¾ cups strawberries
⅓ cup agave syrup
juice of 1 lemon
¼ teaspoon xanthan gum

1. Combine strawberries, agave, lemon juice, and xanthan gum in a blender, and puree until strawberries are crushed.

2. Strain the mixture to remove seeds and transfer to whipped cream dispenser. Load cartridges and set aside in the refrigerator.

To assemble:

chocolate milkshake
cookies and cream milkshake
strawberry foam

1. To the glasses with the chocolate milkshake, carefully pour the cookies-and-cream milkshake on top. Top it off with strawberry foam.

Recipe index